Weekend
Bathroom
Makeovers

Weekend
Bathroom
Makeovers

**Amy Matthews and
Bridget Biscotti Bradley**

LARK BOOKS

A Division of Sterling Publishing Co., Inc.
New York

Series Editor: Dawn Cusick
Managing Editor: Bridget Biscotti Bradley,
Series Designer: Thom Gaines
Art Director: Thom Gaines
Cover Designer: DIY Network
Copy Editor: John Edmonds
Illustrator: Ian Worpole
Editorial Assistance: Laura Del Fava

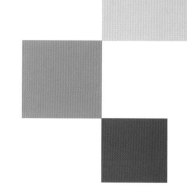

Library of Congress Cataloging-in-Publication Data

Matthews, Amy.
    Weekend bathroom makeovers / Amy Matthews and Bridget Biscotti Bradley.
        p. cm.
    Includes index.
    ISBN-13: 978-1-57990-856-X (pbk.)
    ISBN-10: 1-57990-856-X (pbk.)
    1. Bathrooms–Remodeling–Amateurs' manuals. 2. Interior decoration. I.
Bradley, Bridget Biscotti. II. Title.
    TH4816.3.B37M38 2006
    643'.52–dc22

                                2006003203

10 9 8 7 6 5 4 3 2

Published by Lark Books, A Division of Sterling Publishing Co., Inc.
387 Park Avenue South, New York, N.Y. 10016

Distributed in Canada by Sterling Publishing, c/o Canadian Manda Group, 165 Dufferin Street
Toronto, Ontario, Canada M6K 3H6

Distributed in the United Kingdom by GMC Distribution Services,
Castle Place, 166 High Street, Lewes, East Sussex, England BN7 1XU

Distributed in Australia by Capricorn Link (Australia) Pty Ltd., P.O. Box 704, Windsor, NSW 2756 Australia

If you have questions or comments about this book, please contact:
Lark Books
67 Broadway
Asheville, NC 28801
(828) 253-0467

Manufactured in China

For information about custom editions,
special sales, premium and corporate purchases,
please contact Sterling Special Sales Department
at 800-805-5489 or specialsales@sterlingpub.com.

ISBN 13: 978-1-57990-856-X
ISBN 10: 1-57990-856-0

Contents

What is so special about the bathroom?
It began as a simple space for some of our most basic needs where form followed function. Today, form and function can work together to create not only the necessary ingredients of the bathroom, but a personalized oasis. Our daily lives have gotten hectic, and many of us crave a calm and organized space to prepare for the day ahead, and relax and rejuvenate when the day comes to an end. I'm Amy Matthews, host of DIY's *Bathroom Renovations*, and I want to help you create the sanctuary you've been dreaming of!

We're all looking for something different in our bathrooms. Some of us have limited space to work with but still want a stylish, clean bathroom that's free of those lingering problems we've been looking at for longer than we'd care to admit. Others would love a bathroom with a steam shower; air jetted bath tub; and a floor warming system under natural stone tile.

All of us sit somewhere along this spectrum, and so do our budgets! Remodeling your own bathroom can save you a huge amount of money so you can afford the features you really want. This process is an investment that you can enjoy today, and that will add to the value of your home in the long run. You can't loose. That's the first piece of good news!

The second piece of good news is that, no matter what your level of home improvement skills, this isn't brain surgery. Though there are professionals that should be called in for certain situations (some plumbing, electrical, or a special scenario that you may encounter), so much of the work ahead of you is fun and straightforward once the project gets rolling. From minor repairs and simple updates to creating your dream spa, this book will walk you through the process.

One piece of advice I want to give you is to keep a sense of humor. Things will go wrong! You'll open a wall thinking you're going to find one thing, and you'll encounter an unexpected problem. So when surprises happen, don't let it discourage you; it's just time to move on to plan B.

As you start in on your own bathroom renovation, remember through all the planning, the preparation, the dusty work, the installations, and the finishing touches, you are creating something that is uniquely yours. And when all is said and done, you'll have a great sense of pride in what you've accomplished. Just don't brag too much about how handy you've become, or you might find yourself helping to remodel all of your neighbors' bathrooms!

Amy Matthews,
Host of DIY's Bathroom Renovations

Weekend Bathroom Makeovers

diy network

1

Planning Your Bathroom Renovation

Get out your design hats and your calculator! This is the creative stage where all your ideas start to flow.

What does your bathroom mean to you? It may sound like a silly question, but aside from a few basic needs we all have in common, everyone utilizes their bathroom in a different way. Do you have a small half-bath that you're embarrassed to have guests use when they come over for a party? Do you have a family bathroom that needs to be functional for several people getting ready for school or work at the same time? Do you want a spa getaway where you can relax and retreat from a hectic schedule? Or was your bathroom simply "updated" in a decade you'd rather forget?

Whatever your mission, take the time you need to gather information and materials. Planning your project from start to finish before you begin the construction phase will save you money and headaches in the long run.

In this chapter, you'll learn how to find design inspiration, how to best utilize your budget, and how to decide which parts of the project you should tackle yourself and which ones you should call a professional for. You'll also find great information to help you make decisions on everything from sinks and faucets to floors and finishing touches.

Happy planning!

Getting
STARTED

Spending money on a bathroom remodel is almost always a good investment that will raise your property value. Most often, you'll get 80 to 90 percent of your money back when it comes time to sell the home. With the return on investment so high, there's very little reason to live with a bathroom that you don't like or that is in disrepair. Unless you're thinking about selling your home within the next few years, try not to let the resale value dictate your remodeling decisions. Instead, build a bathroom that will work for your needs and that goes with the style of your house, and you'll be in good shape whether you decide to sell or not.

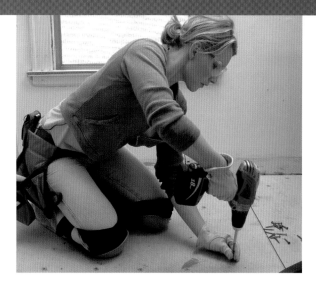

Before you start this or any home improvement project, it pays to have a well-thought-out plan. It may take longer than you'd like to come up with something everyone in the house can agree on, but it's better (and cheaper) to make these decisions up front rather than to change your mind once construction has started.

Renovating a room also requires a detailed plan because the work has to be accomplished in a certain order. Write up a list of all the things you plan to do, such as replace the toilet, remove the existing floor, install a new floor, paint the walls, etc. Next to each task write down whether you have the materials you need now, can get the materials quickly, or need to order in advance. Then make a final list of the order of work, taking labor and materials needs into consideration. After demolition is complete, the best order of work is plumbing or electrical changes, floors, walls, cabinets and counters, new fixtures, and finishing touches.

◄◄ SEEKING INSPIRATION ►►

You may know exactly what you want your new bathroom to look like if you've been dreaming about this project for ages. Or you may never have given bathroom remodeling a thought. The beginning of the project is the time to do your research and think big. Flip through books and magazines. Look at the websites of companies that sell bathroom fixtures. Browse through stores and home improvement centers. Keep a folder of all the pictures, ideas, and advertisements that have caught your eye. Eventually you should start to see a theme emerge. Do all the photos you like show sleek and modern rooms? Is there a color scheme you seem to be drawn to?

Take cues from the style and age of your home. If you live in a house built in the 1920s or 1930s, consider bringing the bathroom back to its original vintage glory. There are many companies that manufacture new period fixtures that look just like

A practical solution can often be made into a focal point. This window adds light to a dark shower area and also adds style to the room (see pages 110-111 for more information).

the originals but utilize modern technology. For example, you can get a claw-foot bathtub that looks like a period piece but is actually a new product with state-of-the-art features.

Tiling is a great job for a patient homeowner to tackle.

CAN I DO THE WORK MYSELF?

Doing the work yourself will give you an amazing sense of pride and accomplishment when the job is done. There's nothing like standing back and admiring the results of a room you've renovated on your own. But at the beginning of a project, the scope of the work may seem daunting. Many people think they need to commit to doing all of the construction work themselves, or none of it. However, you can choose to do some of the work yourself, like demolition, tiling, and painting, and leave less desirable or more complicated jobs to a professional.

Think about how much time you have to devote to this project. If you're remodeling the only bathroom in your house, you'll probably want to finish the project quickly. Unless you're a relatively experienced do-it-yourselfer who owns all the right tools for the job, it may take you two or three times as long to accomplish the same amount of work as a professional. But if you do have another bathroom in the house and enjoy doing the work yourself, you might not mind having this project take up every weekend for the next six weeks.

It can also save you a considerable amount of money to tackle a job yourself. About 25 percent of the cost of a remodel can be attributed to labor—more if you're moving fixtures or structurally changing the room. Those savings can be diminished, however, if you don't already own the tools you'll need. Professionals factor the cost of tools into their bids. Renting tools can save you money but will require time to track down, pick up, clean, and return. You'll also need to be organized and follow a schedule so that you're not paying a day rate on a tool that you're not ready to use.

Cosmetic improvements like installing a new vanity, adding crown molding and paint, and tiling a floor that's in good shape can be accomplished by anyone who has the time and interest to tackle them. If you're adding a large, heavy item like a whirlpool tub or steam shower, you'll need to make sure that your floor is sturdy enough to hold the weight and that your plumbing and electrical systems can support the extra demand. If you're not sure, it's best to hire a professional for those aspects of the job.

TIPS | DIY Network Home Improvement

Building Codes and Permits

Before you start a bathroom renovation, take your drawings to the local building authority and get whatever permits you may need. The authority will be able to tell you whether a permit is required, what part of the work you may have to hire a professional to do, and when the work must be inspected. It is your responsibility to arrange for any required inspections. If the work doesn't meet code or hasn't been inspected, it may need to be ripped out and done over again. Doing work without a permit is illegal and may even invalidate your homeowner's insurance.

Soldering pipes may take some practice, but you'll eventually get the hang of it.

If you can assemble a child's train set, you can install an off-the-shelf cabinet.

If you are leaving major fixtures like the shower, toilet, and sink in the same spots, and if everything is in good working order with no leaks or corrosion, then the remodel will be much more manageable. Anytime you get into rerouting drain and waste lines, adding multiple water supply lines, or moving electrical boxes, a project gets more complicated. That's not to say that homeowners can't do these projects—they absolutely can. But it's better to hire a professional for those parts of the job rather than create future problems with shoddy work if you're not sure how to do them and can't take the time to learn. Be realistic about your skills and time before deciding how you will proceed. Also keep in mind that you will need to get the proper building permits and inspections yourself if you do not hire a contractor.

Hooking up an electrical heating system is best left to professionals.

◢ WANTS VERSUS NEEDS ◣

To help determine whether you can keep your original floor plan or need to change it, make a list of wants versus needs. Are you remodeling a shared bathroom with only one sink? Adding a second sink might then go under your needs list. If you have any water damage or fixtures that don't work properly, those would also fall under the needs category. Would you like to enclose your tub and shower with a glass door? This may be an example of something for the wants list since a shower curtain can serve the same purpose.

If items on your needs list require more space, think about expanding the existing bathroom into an adjoining closet or hallway. Or you may get the room you need simply by removing dividing walls within

the bathroom. Hire an architect or contractor if you decide you need to bump out an exterior wall for the extra room you need, as that decision will also affect your house's foundation and roof line. You may also need to consult a professional if you're working with a room that has ventilation problems or that needs additional windows to bring in more natural light.

Think about the way the current space functions. Can two people use the bathroom at once? If not, perhaps enclosing the shower and toilet in one part of the bathroom makes sense so that a second person can use the vanity and mirror at the same time. Remember to consider every detail, including where the towel racks will go. There should be room for at least two towels within reaching distance of the shower and tub.

Take storage needs into account. If you have other places in the home to store extra towels, cleaning supplies, and toiletries that

you rarely use, then you might not need much storage space in the bathroom. If you need more storage, consider installing a cabinet, a freestanding dresser, or a vanity with under-sink space in addition to the medicine cabinet and small shelves that hold daily necessities.

If small children will be using the bathroom, many safety considerations must be incorporated into your plans. Extra storage space may be needed for the toys that kids will want to use in the tub. Elderly and disabled people also have special needs. Safety bars in the bathtub, a place to sit while showering, and nonslip floors are just some of the features the bathroom will require. See pages 28-29 for more information on children's baths and pages 24-25 for information on universal design.

For more information on this kids bathroom cubby, see page 85.

SAFETY

Follow these guidelines and protect yourself at all times.

◢ Always shut off the power before working on an electrical circuit. Then use a circuit tester to double-check that there is no power coming to the wires before you begin working on them.

◢ Always wear eye protection when using a power tool that may create small pieces that can fly into your eyes.

◢ Wear earplugs when using loud power tools.

◢ Never disturb an area that may contain asbestos. If the area must be disturbed, hire a professional asbestos removal company to deal with it safely.

◢ Protect your back while lifting heavy objects. Use your legs and never twist your back while lifting.

◢ Wear heavy rubber gloves to protect your skin from chemicals.

◢ Test any paint that may have been applied before 1980 for lead before removing it. You can purchase lead test kits from home improvement centers. If you determine there is lead in the paint, wear a respirator, goggles, gloves, and protective clothing when removing it, and seal off the room with plastic sheeting. Then clean the area with a particulate vacuum cleaner designed to remove lead paint. Leave no dust behind. If you have a large amount of lead paint to sand or remove, call a professional.

◢ Wear dust masks when sanding wood surfaces or joint compound. It's often easier to breathe with a respirator rather than a dust mask, and respirators do a better job protecting your lungs from fine dust particles.

Assessing
THE SPACE

At this point in the planning, it's helpful to draw out the space on graph paper and play with various ways you can position each element in the room. Choose an item that will be the focal point of the bathroom. This may be a freestanding tub, a vanity, a mirror, or a piece of art. Make sure the first thing a person sees upon walking into the room or glancing in from the outside is not the toilet. It's best if the toilet is behind a vanity or tub, behind a knee wall, or in an alcove.

A Scale Plan

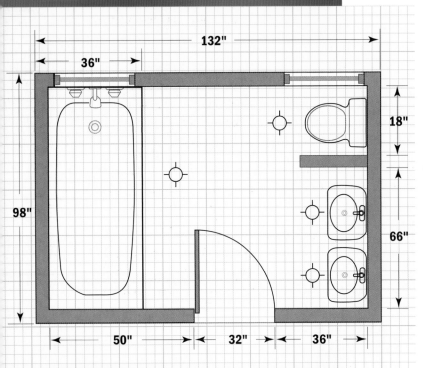

Start by making a rough sketch of your bathroom. It should include architectural elements like doors and windows, electrical receptacles, light fixtures, water supply pipes, and drain pipes. If you know how your pipes run under the floor, include that information as well. If you will be moving supply or drain pipes, you'll be able to use this drawing to show a contractor how far from the main line you want to go.

Once you have a rough sketch, carefully measure the room and use the sketch to note your findings. Don't assume two walls opposite one another are the same size; measure everything twice to be sure you're correct. Measure the floor space in each direction. Then measure the distances from the ground to each plumbing outlet, the distance between the outlets on the walls, and the distance from the corners to these outlets. Note how far up on the wall the electrical receptacles are, and the light fixtures.

SCALE AND ELEVATION PLANS

Transfer the details of your rough sketch to a piece of graph paper and draw the room to scale. Mark permanent architectural items, plumbing, and electrical boxes. Then make about 20 copies of the drawing so you can use it to try out various configurations.

To plan around vertical obstacles in the bathroom, you can make a third type of drawing to show the elevation of a particular wall or walls. It will allow you to see things such as whether a vanity will fit under a window and whether your cabinets are too wide to squeeze between the toilet and tub. Elevations also help you design wall treatments such as tile or wainscoting.

Transfer the measurements of each wall to a new piece of graph paper and mark the locations of receptacles, light fixtures, and plumbing outlets. Then draw in the items you're considering placing on the wall at their appropriate heights and widths. Note which way any cabinet doors hinge open. Move things around until they are arranged in a way that works for your needs and don't block any windows, heat and air vents, etc.

STANDARD MEASUREMENTS

Use the following guidelines from the National Kitchen and Bath Association when planning for your bathroom remodel. Your local code may differ from these measurements in some instances, so be sure to consult those codes before drawing up your final plan.

Door The clear opening of a doorway should be at least 32".

Clear space There should be at least 30" of clear floor space in front of all fixtures and between these fixtures and opposite fixtures, walls, or obstacles.

Single lavatory The distance from the center of the lavatory to a sidewall or tall obstacle should be at least 20".

Double lavatory The distance between the centers of two lavatories should be at least 36".

Lavatory/vanity height The height for a lavatory can vary between 32" and 43", depending on the height of the user.

Shower size The interior of the shower should be at least 36" x 36".

Shower controls The shower controls should be accessible from both inside and outside the shower spray and be located between 38" and 48" above the floor, depending on the user's height.

Tub controls The tub controls should be accessible from both inside and outside the tub and be located between the rim of the bathtub and 33" above the floor.

Toilet/bidet placement The distance from the center lof the toilet and/or bidet to any bath fixture, wall, or other obstacle should be at least 18".

Toilet compartment The size for a separate toilet compartment should be at least 36" x 66" with a swing-out or pocket door.

Electrical receptacles GFCI receptacles should be located at all electrical appliance points of use.

Lighting In addition to general lighting, task lighting should be provided for each functional area in the bathroom (e.g., grooming, showering).

Ventilation Plan a mechanical exhaust system, vented to the outside, for each enclosed area.

When to
HIRE HELP

If you have the time and interest, there is no part of remodeling a bathroom that you can't learn how to do yourself. As long as you apply for and meet the requirements of building permits and inspections, you shouldn't be doing anything that will cause harm to your home. If your bathroom remodel will be merely cosmetic, meaning that no walls or fixtures will be moved, you won't even need to gain proficiency in framing, plumbing, and electrical work.

Renovating an old window requires specific tools most homeowners don't have.

Often it's not a question of ability but one of time. If you have a full-time job, including children to take care of, you may not have the time to dedicate to this type of large project. Bathrooms are also necessities in a home, and if you're remodeling your only one, you'll need to move quickly to avoid displacing yourself and your family for a long time. People who have one or more additional bathrooms in the home have the luxury of being able to pace their remodels a little more slowly.

And then there's the question of tools. Look at the list of things you plan to do in the bathroom and figure out whether you have the equipment to do them right. You can rent tools if you don't own them, but buying a large amount of new equipment that you don't plan on needing again might not be a wise use of money.

Think about which parts of the project you're unsure of how to do, can't do quickly enough, or don't have the tools for, and consider hiring out those portions of the job.

Tasks that require more specific skills and an understanding of local building codes include moving fixtures like toilets or showers (because they require rerouting plumbing supply and drain lines), moving and adding walls, and adding vents that run through the roof. If you hire a contractor for these aspects of the job, he or she can handle the permit and inspection process for you and free up your time to focus on planning and executing other parts of the job.

◀ STRUCTURAL CHANGES ▶

Sometimes it's just not possible to turn your existing bathroom into one that suits your needs without adding more square footage. This will involve either taking space from an adjoining room or closet, or adding on to the house. Both solutions will significantly raise the cost of your bathroom remodel, although bumping out will cost more because it requires a new foundation and an extension of the roofline.

Before you start tearing down walls to extend the bathroom into an adjoining space, you need to be sure they aren't load bearing. A load-bearing wall helps to hold the weight of the roof or the floor above. Load-bearing walls will often be stacked one on top of another, from the basement to the attic. If you don't know for sure that a wall is not load bearing, you need to consult an architect or engineer.

Tearing down walls means that you'll probably be building new ones as well. This job requires some basic framing, insulating, and finishing know-how. If you're not up to learning how to do this, hire it out and keep your focus on the finish work.

TIPS | DIY Network Home Improvement

Getting Bids

If you do decide to hire out any portion of your remodel, make sure you get at least three bids from three different contractors. Ask each contractor for two to four references from jobs they recently completed and call those homeowners to get a better sense of whether or not each contractor will do a good job for you.

VENTILATION

It's crucial that bathrooms be well ventilated. Plan to add an exhaust fan during your remodel if for some reason you don't already have one. Moist air needs to be drawn out of the room or it will seriously damage walls and fixtures over time.

Most building codes require proper ventilation in a bathroom, either through windows, skylights that open and close, or an exhaust fan. The problem with relying on windows to ventilate the bath is that people either forget to open and close them or don't want to let cold air in. So it's better to just install an exhaust fan to protect your bathroom from moisture damage on a daily basis. To make sure fans can do their job, leave them on for 20 minutes after your shower. Put the system on a timer so you won't have to watch the clock.

Exhaust fans need to be vented out through the wall or the roof. Consider hiring a professional to install one for you if you don't already have the venting in place. All exhaust fans have CFM ratings, which stands for cubic feet per minute. This measurement tells you how many cubic feet of air they can move in a minute at a given pressure. To figure out what CFM rating you need, multiply the total cubic footage of the room by the height of the ceiling in feet and then divide that number by 60. Bathrooms over 100 square feet should have at least 50 CFMs for each basic fixture. You'll need more if you have fixtures that put out a lot of steam, like a jetted tub or a shower with multiple spray jets. If you have a steam shower, that will need its own dedicated exhaust fan.

BUDGET

Making a budget will help you further refine your list of wants and needs. It's a good idea to come up with a figure you're willing to spend on this project, including any parts that you may decide to hire out, before making final decisions on fixtures and materials. Never try to save money on systems such as plumbing and electrical. If you need to update your pipes, add a shutoff valve, fix a leak, install new receptacles, or add better ventilation, these are the things you can't skimp on. Why build a gorgeous new bathroom with beautiful wall tiles if you'll have to tear through them in a couple of years to fix a leaking pipe?

SAVING MONEY

The national average for the cost of a bathroom remodel is $10,000. You can add a new vanity, tile the floor, and update fixtures and accessories for much less than that, especially if you do the work yourself. If you're adding square footage, moving walls or plumbing fixtures, installing spa-type fixtures like a steam shower, or if you decide to cover every inch of the floor and walls with Italian travertine tile, the price can well exceed $10,000. Use your scale drawings to determine how much your materials will cost by the square foot, and then consider using less costly materials for some areas if you're going over budget.

One sure-fire way to save money is to make a plan and stick to it. If you decide on one configuration, get halfway done with the job, and then change your mind, you will loose money. Likewise if you buy and install a certain kind of tile or fixture, then decide to go another direction with the style of the room. Take as much time as you need to research your decisions so you feel confident about them before you begin the construction phase.

You can often save large amounts of money by choosing standard, mass-produced materials and colors over custom designs and rare materials. For example, a basic chrome faucet bought from a home improvement center can cost around $80, while one plated with nickel in a vintage design can cost several hundred. Resilient flooring like vinyl will cost less than ceramic tile, and ceramic

Use more expensive glass tiles as accents instead of covering the whole wall with them.

tile will cost less than stone. Buying a basic fiberglass bathtub or refinishing your existing tub costs a fraction of what a freestanding jetted tub will. Decide on the parts of the bathroom that are most important to you and make compromises in other areas.

Doing the work yourself will save you a considerable amount of money, as the labor costs for time-intensive projects like tiling and plumbing are so high. It could be that by doing your own installation you will be able to afford nicer materials and fixtures. If your budget is not that tight, consider splurging on high-end materials or one great fixture that you'll be particularly proud of and that will set your bathroom apart from the rest.

HEATING SOLUTIONS

Some bathrooms are hooked into the house's heating system and already have a register in place. But in older homes and those without a whole-house heating system, the bathroom can be a cold place in winter. If you lack bathroom heat, here are some options.

Space heaters. Be sure you buy a space heater that's rated for bathroom use and includes an ALCI safety plug, which prevents shock in case the unit comes into contact with water. It's also a good idea to choose one that shuts itself off after a certain amount of time. Fan heaters reduce the steam produced in a bathroom by raising the ambient temperature closer to that of the hot water. Small rooms can be warmed quickly with this method, and they'll stay dryer. Heat lamps don't heat the whole room as well since they aren't heating the air, just the objects they are near. Place them high up in the room so the warm air will reach your whole body.

Floor warming systems. Radiant heat warming systems will take the chill off a cold floor. Wire mats are stapled down to the subfloor, and mortar or a thin coat of concrete can be installed right over them. You can buy these systems off the shelf and install the wires on the floor, but it's recommended that an electrician come and do the final hookups. Don't install a radiant heat floor warming system under wood or resilient floors. They are meant for ceramic tile, stone, carpet, and poured concrete floors.

Universal DESIGN

Before a bathroom remodel is a great time to think about incorporating universal design features. If you plan on living in your home into retirement years, this can be a practical decision. But even if you're young and healthy, it's wise to consider universal design principles so that whoever eventually moves into or visits your home will be able to use the bathroom safely.

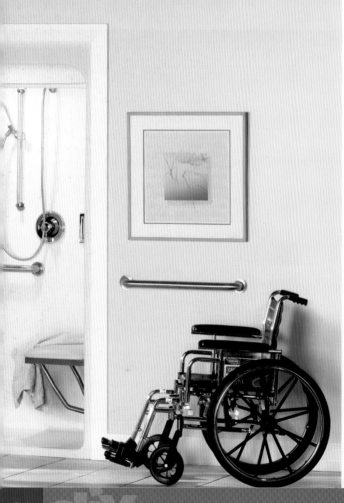

UNIVERSAL DESIGN FEATURES

Homes with universal design features include those that are all one level with no stairs to the main entrance or between rooms. Doorways are 32" to 36" wide and hallways are 36" to 42" wide to accommodate wheelchairs. In the bathroom, floors and bathtubs have nonslip surfaces, handrails, and thresholds that are flush with the floor. Lever door handles make opening and closing doors easier for people with reduced hand strength.

If you really want to make it easy for people in wheelchairs or those with limited mobility to use the bathroom, design one with a barrier-free shower. The bathroom floor will need to slope toward a center drain so that water doesn't go where it shouldn't. Even if no one with a disability currently uses the bathroom, many people choose this kind of shower for its sleek, open look.

The Americans With Disabilities Act provides the following additional guidelines for bathrooms:

There should be at least 5' of clearance in the room so wheelchairs can make a 180-degree turn. Or you can design the bathroom in a T-shape with each part of the T at least 36" wide so the wheelchair can make a three-point turn.

Accessible toilets have seats that are 17" to 19" off the floor.

The rim of the sink should be no higher than 34" off the floor. Sinks should extend 17" from the rear wall, and the space under the sink needs to be open so a wheelchair can slide under it, with a clearance of at least 29" from the floor to the bottom of the sink. Protective covers should be installed over the water supply lines so that legs aren't scalded by hot pipes. Faucets should be single-lever models.

A person in a wheelchair can roll right up to this vanity, and the towel on the front-mounted bar is easily accessible.

A sloped floor prevents water from the open shower from traveling over to the bath area.

Grab bars should be placed horizontally behind and to the side of the toilet, and inside bathtubs and showers. These bars need to be attached to studs inside the wall. Consider placing the reinforcements inside the walls when remodeling the bath and installing the bars later if they aren't needed now.

Choose nonslip floor surfaces. Large tiles with a slight texture and few grout lines are a good choice, as is sheet vinyl.

Add an integrated bench in the shower.

Choose handheld showerheads to more easily wash children and keep certain areas on older or injured people dry if need be.

Replace toggle switches with large rocker plates.

Place towel bars and robe hooks lower on the wall where children and people in wheelchairs can reach them.

Types of
BATHROOMS

From powder rooms to shared baths to luxury master suites, each bathroom in the house has its own unique set of standards and needs. Think about the space you're remodeling and how it might be used before deciding on style and materials.

◢ MASTER BATHROOMS ◣

An adult-only sanctuary, the master bath is generally a large space located next to or off of the master bedroom. Small master baths consist of a shower or shower-tub combo, two sinks, and a toilet. Those that have the extra space can incorporate luxurious amenities such as saunas, bidets, jetted or soaking tubs, and large showers with two or more shower-heads. Some master baths also have space for a dressing table, walk-in closets, and built-in cabinets for storing clothes or linens.

Large bathrooms require special planning in the layout stage. If you're remodeling a master bath, consider the needs of all people who will be using the space. Try to put the sinks 3 feet apart so there is enough room for two people to maneuver. Include one large mirror over the vanity so you don't need to jockey for position. And consider putting the toilet in an alcove so that another person can use the vanity or tub at the same time.

If you have an older home with a small master bath and want to enlarge the space, look for opportunities to expand into adjacent bedrooms or closets or even into the master bedroom itself if necessary. Keep in mind that high-end fixtures like soaking tubs and saunas require strong floors. If you aren't sure that the older floors in your home can handle the weight, hire a contractor to reinforce them.

SHARED BATHROOMS

If there's only one bathroom in the house, it's by default a shared bath. You may have one full bathroom off the master bedroom plus a half-bath or powder room near the living area, in which case you may call it a shared bath or a master bath. Shared bathrooms are used by two or more adults, or a combination of adults and children.

Because shared bathrooms need to function efficiently for multiple people, perhaps at the same time, layout and storage are the main things to consider during a remodel. If the existing space has only one sink, try to find a way to add a second one. A dual vanity with cabinet space underneath will solve both the sink and storage dilemma, although large cabinets can sometimes overwhelm small spaces. Consider using two pedestal sinks and a freestanding cabinet in a corner of the room for a more open feel. Try to provide privacy so that multiple people can use the bathroom at once. For example, choose a glass surround for the bath or shower that you can't see through. Put the toilet in a separate alcove, behind a knee wall, or behind a partition screen.

It can be challenging to find space to hang more than two full-size towels. If you're short on empty wall space, use hooks instead of towel bars and put them in alternating rows high and low on the wall. Adults and older children can use the tall hooks, and smaller children will be able to reach the low ones.

Shared bathrooms are often placed between two bedrooms. During your bathroom remodel, consider taking the room down to the studs so you can install acoustical insulation in the walls. This way, people who are sleeping in adjoining rooms won't be woken up by the sounds of running water in the morning.

◢ KIDS' BATHROOMS ◣

Bathrooms that will be used by children need to incorporate a variety of safety features. Those that are devoted solely to children can undergo a major transformation, like the one shown on pages 76-85, including a lowered vanity and a kid-size toilet. But those that are shared baths can still be made kid-friendly with the right materials and fixtures.

◢ Install a slip-resistant floor. Sheet vinyl or vinyl tiles are the best choices, followed by ceramic tiles with a texture or very small tiles with a lot of grout lines.

◢ Install safety latches on cabinet doors and don't store toxic or dangerous items at ground level.

◢ Make sure countertops and tubs have rounded edges.

◢ Choose a shower curtain instead of glass doors around a tub and shower combination, as it will be easier to reach in and assist young bathers. If you do have a glass shower door, make sure it's tempered so that the glass won't shatter if it breaks.

◢ Buy a new bathtub with a textured surface, or use textured bath mats in your existing tub.

◢ Put a rubber protector over the tub's faucet to avoid bumps and bruises. Protectors come in a variety of shapes and colors.

◢ Make sure the tub and shower have scald-free valves.

◢ Put childproof covers on all receptacles and make sure there are no hanging cords coming from hair dryers or window treatments that kids can get tangled up in.

If there's room for two vanities, hang one a little lower on the wall for young children to reach. Otherwise, make sure there's a footstool for them to climb up on when using the sink. Kid-size toilets install the same way as regular models and can be swapped out when the little ones outgrow it.

Whatever kind of toilet you choose, make sure you install a toilet lid lock so that toddlers and their toys won't fall in.

Provide open cubbies to encourage kids to put away their own toys, and hooks lower to the ground so they can hang up their own towels. Look for a shower curtain with breathable pockets that kids can use to store toys and shampoo.

◢ POWDER ROOMS ◣

Bathrooms that do not include showers or bathtubs are often called half-baths or powder rooms. Typically used by guests, they are often quite small and barely have room for a toilet and small sink. But their small size can be an advantage when you're remodeling, as you will be able to afford finer materials in smaller quantities.

Consider replacing a standard swing-out door with a pocket door to save space. Sometimes the powder room is so small that you have to maneuver yourself around the door to get it closed. The downside of a pocket door is that it cuts down on the soundproofing of the room.

Some powder rooms are built without proper ventilation. Although there is no shower, steam can still come from the sink. If there is no window, invest in a bathroom fan during the remodel.

Choose a sleek, space-efficient vanity. If you don't need the storage space, a pedestal sink will visually open up the room. It's still a good idea to have a little counter space for guests to put their purses on or for soap and a flower vase. If your pedestal sink doesn't have enough flat surface area on the edges, put small shelves on the wall or

recessed between wall studs. This is also a good solution if you decide on a truly minimal floating sink and wall-mounted faucet.

Don't be afraid to add a punchy color to the walls. If you choose a bright or warm color it shouldn't make the space feel any smaller. Finish the room off with an interesting light fixture, coordinated accessories, a framed mirror, and soft towels.

◢ HOME SPAS ◣

For people who enjoy the occasional spa treatment, turning their own master bathroom into a spa bath is the ultimate indulgence. This type of bathroom remodel will be more expensive not only because of higher-end fixtures but because heavy items like soaking tubs and steam showers need strong floors, added electrical circuits, and larger hot-water tanks. As you begin to plan for a spa bath, be sure to factor in the cost of updating the structure of your floor as well as the electrical and plumbing systems.

Bathtubs

Upgrading to a jetted tub used to be the mark of a luxury bathroom. Today, you can also find bathtubs with tiny holes along the bottom edge that create small, soft champagne bubbles rather than blasting you with water jets. Soaking tubs are another newly popular option. These large, often self-standing tubs can sometimes accommodate two people. Certain models have an enclosure for spillover water so that you can literally sit in a tub that's full to the brim and not worry about getting the floor wet.

Inspired by hotel spas with outdoor rooms, homeowners are also choosing to install large tubs on an enclosed deck or patio right off the master bathroom. Consider this option if you live in a temperate climate and could enjoy bathing en plain aire for at least part of the year.

Handheld faucets are perfect companions to large bathtubs. For self-standing tubs, faucets can

relaxing foot massage while you enjoy your steam. There are also steam shower heads with a compartment for essential oils that are slowly emitted along with the steam. For people who appreciate the effects of chromatherapy (light therapy), choose a steam showerhead that can color the water as it spills over you. Warm colors stimulate and cool colors calm your nerves. See this option in action in the high-tech bathroom renovation on pages 136-147.

Ambiance

Choose earth tones and warm colors to decorate your spa bathroom. Live plants, bamboo mats, and natural stone can bring the outdoors in. White and blue glass will reflect the light and make for a watery atmosphere. Pay attention to your lighting plan as well. Put overhead lights on dimmer switches, with task lighting near the vanity and a collection of candles near the tub. Add a sound system so you can listen to relaxing music while you soak in your tub. You can buy wireless speakers that stick to the outside of the tub, or plan for speakers to be installed in the ceiling or walls if you're doing a major remodel.

come up through the floor and rest on the edge. There are also tall and wide faucets that allow water to come pouring into the tub for a waterfall effect.

Showers

To give your existing shower a spa makeover, try adding an oversized showerhead or one that sits in the middle of the ceiling and spills soft streams of water over a large area. If you're starting from scratch and can make some plumbing additions, add a second showerhead above or below your existing one, or to the other side of the shower. You can also install body jets so that strong sprays of water will hit you at various points for a full-body massage. Most models include between 4 and 10 vertically mounted jets.

Part of the spa experience for many people is sitting in a luxurious steam room while waiting for their massage or facial appointment. Steam showers can also be installed in your home bathroom. If you go this route, consider including a bench in your design. Some steam shower models include jets around the edge of the basin so you can have a

Bathroom STYLE

Now that you've decided on the size and scope of your bathroom remodel it's time for the fun, creative, and sometimes overwhelming tasks of coming up with a style for the room and deciding on fixtures and materials. Be prepared to make compromises and change your mind as you go through this process as you'll likely stumble across some options you didn't know exist. First, the big-picture question: What style of room are you going for?

Contemporary

Victorian

You've probably already started this process by looking at books and magazines and in coming up with the layout of your new bathroom. You may have a specific look that you're trying to adhere to, perhaps one based on the style of the rest of your home, such as traditional, modern, or arts and crafts. Or there may not be one term that defines the look you're going for. You may simply be drawn to a certain color scheme or want a formal or informal space. Or you may have chosen one fixture that will define the style of the rest of the room. If you aren't sure what the main characteristics of certain styles are, here's a basic rundown.

Traditional

A traditional bathroom incorporates rich materials such as gold and silk. It includes all the standard amenities but nothing novel or high tech. The room has vivid or sophisticated color combinations and a comfortable feel. More elaborate wall treatments and patterns may be used, such as printed wallpaper in strong colors, and wainscoting.

Country

A handcrafted, casual look that incorporates printed fabrics, light-colored woods such as pine or oak, painted or distressed furniture, and perhaps antique décor or wall art. Floral patterns, cheerful colors, and hand-woven rugs work well in this style of bathroom.

Victorian

A feminine style that utilizes printed fabrics, fringes, and tassels. You may find an overstuffed chair or footstool next to a stand-alone claw-foot tub sitting under a window with lace curtains. Lots of knickknacks in crystal, silver, and gold.

Contemporary

This is a high tech look with clean lines and a soft color palette, perhaps with a bright or punchy color to accent one wall or area. Utilizes sleek fixtures and prefabricated vanities and storage cabinets. Minimalist, clutter-free, and clean with lots of glass and metal.

Arts and Crafts

Uses geometric patterns to ornament natural materials such as wood, stone, and concrete. An earth-toned color scheme and fixtures that have strong lines and angles. Metals include copper and bronze, and wood is generally stained a dark color.

Traditional/Country

Arts and Crafts

Period

You can get a period look either by shopping for antiques and original fixtures or by buying newly made fixtures with modern technology that look like original pieces. Period reproductions are well crafted and solid. Any period can be mimicked, including vintage turn of the century, art deco, or the 1950s. Some people even choose to re-create a 1970s bathroom complete with pea-green tub and toilet.

Modern

Based on the principle that form follows function. Bathrooms utilize steel, plastics, laminated woods, and fiberglass. Bold, primary colors are used, and there is a minimalist, uncluttered look to the room.

Period

Modern

◀ COLOR ▶

You can also start your bathroom design with a basic color scheme and see where that leads you. Some people are afraid of color. If you've always had white walls but are up to trying a color or two, the bathroom is a great place to experiment.

While it's true that light colors make a room feel larger and dark colors can sometimes close a room in, there really shouldn't be any color that's off-limits in the bathroom as long as it's used with some restraint. For example, dark colors like chocolate brown can be used successfully in small rooms. Consider painting one or two walls brown and use white, cream, or robin's-egg blue on the other two walls. Or use light tiles halfway up the wall, or wainscoting, and paint the rest

of the wall a dark color. Top it off with white crown molding and a white pedestal sink and the dark color will add punch to the room.

The use of color can really affect your mood. Bathrooms used as retreats should have relaxing combinations such as blues, neutrals like creams and tans, or colors found in nature. If you have trouble waking up, perhaps a bright orange or lime green would get you moving during your morning routine.

Choose a palette of three to six colors and use those for the floors, walls, trim, and accessories such as towels. Then pick white porcelain, metal, or glass fixtures. If you have a hard time deciding which colors work well

together, then stick with one color and white. Black and white together are a classic look. Add red or yellow hand towels for a little personality. Blue and white always work well in a watery environment like the bathroom. You may venture out and use one shade of blue for the walls and another for the floors. Pastel colors like light pink or pale green also work well with white or cream accents. You really can't go wrong by mixing any one color with white.

Also consider your own habits for cleaning the bathroom. Don't use white floor tiles and light wall and countertop colors if you have kids in the house or don't get around to cleaning it often enough. Dark colors will do a better job of hiding scuff marks, stains, and dirt.

FLOORS

Whatever flooring material you decide to go with, make sure that it will stand up to moisture and that it's not terribly slippery when wet. Some flooring is more suitable for bathrooms than others. Consider your space and who uses it when selecting this important component.

Vinyl

Marble tiles

Hardwood

VINYL

There are many positive aspects of a vinyl bathroom floor. It's relatively simple to install (especially if you have a flat and sound subfloor), it resists water damage, it's available in textures that are slip resistant, and it's one of the least expensive flooring choices. It does require some basic upkeep, though. If you don't buy prewaxed vinyl, then you should seal it regularly, especially if you have sheet vinyl with a seam or vinyl tiles. If the edges aren't sealed, water can seep in and damage your subfloor. Some vinyl can discolor when exposed to sunlight, and some can be punctured by sharp objects or heavy furniture.

CERAMIC TILE

Tile is a durable flooring material for the bathroom because it's naturally resistant to water and stains. It comes in an incredible array of colors and shapes. Handmade tiles with special finishes like glaze or crackle will cost more than machine-made ones. Choose small tiles for the bathroom so that you have enough grout lines to make the floor less slippery when wet. Or you can find ceramic tiles with a light texture if you prefer large blocks of tile and fewer grout lines. Be sure to seal the grout so it doesn't get stained.

STONE

An elegant, high-end choice, stone works beautifully in the bathroom and can be well worth the high price. Pick a textured or honed stone finish rather than a smooth and glossy one for better slip resistance. Stain them to keep out moisture and dirt. Marble can be cold and slippery, and it's heavy enough that you'll need to be sure your subfloor can take the weight. Slate is naturally textured and water resistant, making it a good choice for very wet areas like the shower.

WOOD

If you have hardwood floors in the rest of your house, it may be tempting to install one in the bathroom as well. Wood can't be beat for a warm, comfortable look. However, you're risking big problems if the bathroom should ever flood. Hardwood won't be able to recover from that kind of water damage. It may also shrink and expand just from the moisture in the air. If you do choose a hardwood floor, make sure it is well sealed at all times. A safer option is wood laminate, which is easier to maintain. It comes prefinished and sealed, and you can replace a strip if it becomes damaged. Ask about the water-resistant properties of the brand you want to buy.

RESILIENT

Natural materials like linoleum and cork fall under this category. Linoleum is resistant to bacteria and has antistatic properties that repel dust and grime, making it an excellent choice for the bathroom. Cork is anti-microbial but not water resistant and needs to be kept sealed. Both are quiet and warm underfoot.

CONCRETE

Concrete is fast becoming a popular choice in modern and contemporary homes. It's obviously hard to damage and easy to clean. Decorative concrete techniques can be utilized for color and pattern. It's downsides are that it's cold and hard on your feet, although you can install electric in-floor heat systems underneath to warm it up. It should be sealed regularly to repel stains.

CARPET

There's nothing warmer or softer underfoot than carpet, and it's available in any color and pattern under the sun. Carpet is a better choice for powder rooms than for bathrooms with tubs or showers because it absorbs water, promotes mildew growth, and is hard to clean. If you must have carpet, choose nylon or other synthetic materials in a short pile. An even better choice is woven vinyl sisal, which is water and stain resistant.

Concrete

Woven vinyl sisal

WALLS

You can use practically any material that will stand up to moisture and steam on your bathroom walls. Here's what you need to know about the most popular options.

Wallpaper

Wood wainscotting

PAINT

No other wall covering can dramatically transform the look of a room as easily, quickly, and inexpensively as paint. Semigloss and satin finishes will be easier to clean than flat paints. High gloss offers the most moisture resistance, but some people don't like the shiny look and it can also accentuate imperfections in the wall.

WALLPAPER

Buy high-quality vinyl wallpaper for the bathroom. Other types may not fare well in moist environments but would be suitable in powder rooms or bathrooms that aren't used frequently.

WAINSCOTING

Wood wainscoting is a beautiful way to protect your walls and add some architectural detail to the bathroom. If you use real wood, it should be primed and painted on both sides to help prevent moisture damage and reduce swelling. A good alternative is MDF wainscoting, which fares better in moist areas and comes with tongue-and-groove edges, which make it easier to put together. Most MDF is bonded with urea formaldehyde, which can release toxic fumes into your home for months. Look for MDF that uses no added formaldehyde; it can be specially ordered through green building supply companies.

Ceramic wall tile

CERAMIC TILE

You'll have more choices in styles and colors of ceramic tile for walls than you will for floors, as they don't have to be able to withstand as much use. Tiles are water resistant and can add color and texture to the walls. You can use tile as baseboard for the bottom 4 or 8 inches of the wall, or use it as wainscoting and bring it up to chair-rail height. If you have a pedestal sink, consider tiling behind it from the floor up to about 6 inches above the faucet as a large backsplash.

STONE

You can purchase large slabs of stone to use as wainscoting, but the weight and expense of stone slabs make them unrealistic for most bathroom remodels. Look for man-made replicas like cultured marble (see page 96), or stick with stone tiles for the walls instead. Unlike for the floor, you can choose smooth and glossy stone tiles since you won't have to worry about them being slippery.

Travertine stone tile

CABINETS

Bathroom cabinets look a lot like kitchen cabinets, but they serve different purposes. In the bathroom, you need to store large and bulky items like towels as well as small bottles of lotions and potions. If you're renovating a shared bath, you'll want enough cabinet space for each person to have his or her own shelf or drawer.

Using prefabricated stock cabinets is a good way to save money if by now you've blown your budget on a few fancy fixtures. Cabinets that you can buy off the shelf are 30" or 32" tall, but you can get them 36" or higher if you need more space. They generally increase in 3" or 6" increments. Standard depths are between 18" and 24". Deeper cabinets will provide more storage and counter area, if you have the extra floor space. You'll generally be able to find stock cabinets for the vanity and for tall storage cabinets, corner cabinets, and wall-hung cabinets.

You can make stock cabinets look more custom by adding trim. Choose a style that goes with or matches the trim around windows and doors in the bathroom. Some stock cabinetry comes with fill pieces so that you can hide the space between the wall and where the cabinet starts if you need to work around an obstacle or need room for a door or drawer to open.

Choices beyond stock cabinetry include semicustom cabinets, which are built to your specifications and can incorporate custom storage options; and custom cabinets, which can be made to fit any space, as they are usually constructed on site by a carpenter.

Whether you go with stock, semicustom, or custom, you will need to choose between face-frame and frameless styles. Traditional face frames, also called American-style, have 1-by-2 boards on the front of the doors and drawers, and the door hinges are usually visible. European frameless cabinets have doors and drawers that cover almost all of the front surface area of the cabinet, and door hardware is invisible when the doors are closed. They offer a more contemporary look.

Stock cabinets with a thermofoil laminate finish

Antique dresser/vanity

TYPES OF WOOD

Solid-wood cabinets are beautiful but are prone to warping in moist areas like a bathroom. If you decide to go with them anyway, make sure every inch is sealed with marine-grade urethane sealant or paint. If you want painted cabinets, though, go with something other than solid wood. Laminates have three layers (including the color or print and a sealant) that are fused over a particleboard or plywood carcass. Cabinets with laminate exteriors will fare well in the bathroom. Another good option is veneered cabinets, which have a thin layer of real wood over plywood or another inexpensive base material. With this option you can get the look of solid wood without risking damage from the moisture and humidity.

SIGNS OF A WELL-MADE CABINET

The best-made cabinets are constructed with dowels and screws or dovetail joinery. If you choose wood cabinets, make sure the seams between one piece of veneer and the next are not noticeable. Drawers should have four sides with a separate face piece fastened to the front of the box. They should open and close smoothly and have invisible, under-mounted runners. All joints should be tight, and topcoat finishes should be smooth.

FURNITURE

In period bathrooms, stock cabinetry can look odd. If you don't want a pedestal sink and stand-alone shelves, you can look for a piece of antique furniture to turn into a bathroom vanity. You will most likely need to remove the top piece and replace it with a custom countertop with a hole for the sink. You'll also need to make some cutouts in the back and the drawers to fit the plumbing inside. See pages 100-101 to learn how to turn an antique dresser into a vanity. Or combine a pedestal sink with a tall antique dresser that can hold towels and toiletries.

Dovetail joinery

COUNTERTOPS

There are many choices in countertop materials for the bathroom, and the decision usually comes down to style versus budget. In general, what works for the kitchen will work for the bath. It's important that the countertop be easy to clean and able to take some hard hits and standing water. The least expensive options are ceramic tile, plastic laminate, and wood, all of which should be well under $50 per running foot (meaning the distance from one end of the countertop to the other). Synthetic stone and stone tiles will run between $50 and $80 per running foot, and higher-end options like solid-surface and stone slabs can cost between $100 and $250 per running foot.

Laminate

▰ CERAMIC TILE ▰

It can be tempting to cover your bathroom countertop with ceramic tile if you also have tile floors or walls to create a unified look. Ceramic tile comes in a wide variety of colors, sizes, and designs, and it can take a lot of abuse. Even though you don't need to choose hardy ceramic tiles rated for floor use, it's wise to stay away from glass or other delicate tiles on the countertop just in case something heavy falls on them. You can always find a coordinating tile for the countertop and use art tiles on the backsplash. Just as on the floor, you need to keep the grout sealed so that dirt, stains, and mold don't discolor it.

▰ PLASTIC LAMINATE ▰

Laminate is a popular choice in the bathroom because it's inexpensive, durable, and available in every color and pattern you can imagine. The laminate is glued to a substrate like fiberboard, and it can be bought either off the shelf or custom, meaning you can get more interesting designs and edge treatments. The downside of laminate is that if you do happen to chip, stain, or scratch it, you'll have to replace the whole countertop. It can also burn, and the color can dull over time.

Solid surface

▰ SOLID SURFACE ▰

Popular in kitchens, solid surface is also a good choice for the bathroom because it requires little maintenance and it's hard to damage. Solid surface is commonly available in light colors with speckles. You can also find types that look like marble or granite. It can be a good choice for odd-shaped bathrooms because the acrylic resin material can be molded into any shape. Most types require professional installation.

Integral sink

options, but they need to be polished regularly to maintain their shine. If you don't polish them, they will oxidize, which is a look some people may prefer. All metals are prone to scratches.

CONCRETE

More companies are offering do-it-yourself concrete countertop kits these days. Concrete looks great in both natural and high-tech bathrooms. You can get creative by coloring and stamping the concrete, but keep it well sealed to avoid staining. Hairline cracks are often part of the look.

STONE

It's hard to beat stone for elegance and style, and it is durable, water resistant, and heatproof. The only downside to marble, limestone, and granite is that they can be stained if not regularly sealed. Stone slabs are expensive, but you can sometimes find remnant pieces to fit smaller vanities. If you want natural stone but a solid slab is beyond your budget, choose stone tiles instead. Synthetic marble and granite bathroom counters that you can find at home centers look a lot like the real thing and will stand up to oils, alcohol, and harsh cleaners, while unsealed natural stone does not.

WOOD

Nothing beats the warmth of wood, but it needs to be sealed with a polyurethane or marine varnish if you want it in the bathroom. It's better kept to the part of the vanity that's not near the sink. If you do put it around the sink, be sure the edges are well sealed so that water doesn't rot it from the inside. A high-sheen varnish will make it easier to clean.

Stone tile

INTEGRAL SINK

A countertop with an integrated sink is a good choice for bathrooms used by kids. There's no sink rim or joints for dirt to get trapped in, and the edges can be rounded to prevent bumps and bruises. They can be made to fit any size vanity and come in a variety of colors. Some manufacturers provide repair kits just in case the material gets scratched or stained.

METAL

If you want a modern-looking bathroom and you're rigorous about cleaning up watermarks, consider a stainless-steel countertop. Buy a chromium and nickel blend that's 16-gauge or higher. Lesser metals are prone to staining. Copper and zinc are also

SINKS

Most people choose their countertop first and then buy a sink that will work with it, making this decision more of an afterthought. But you might have strong feelings about how the sink is set (either above, at, or below the countertop) that can affect your countertop decision. Or you may either prefer the look of or have room for only a pedestal or wall-mounted sink, which means you can forgo the countertop decision altogether. Basic deck-mounted sinks cost around $100, while pedestal sinks can cost several hundred depending on the design. For art glass sinks, sculptural stand-alone basins, and rare materials, the cost could go into the thousands.

Self-rimming

DECK-MOUNTED

This category includes drop-in models made to fit inside the countertop cutout; self-rimming, which overlap the counter surface; undermount, which are recessed below the counter; and vessel, which sit on top of the counter.

Undermounts are easier to clean but cost more than drop-in and self-rimming. Vessel sinks can cost more than $1,000 because they are often artistically designed and made of interesting materials like copper or glass.

Undermount

PEDESTAL

Pedestal sinks are good choices for period remodels, powder rooms, and any bathroom where space is at a premium. You can buy small models with no counter space or larger ones with enough space to hold a few items on either side of the sink. Your plumbing will be exposed, so choosing a pedestal sink can also mean rerouting or replacing pipes and hardware. It's also best to mount a pedestal sink to a stud or piece of wood placed horizontally in the wall, so it requires some up-front planning.

Console sinks look a lot like pedestal sinks, but instead of one center support they have two or four thin legs. The sink is attached to the wall and provides more counter space than traditional pedestal sinks. These are often available only by special order.

Vessel

Pedestal

WALL-MOUNTED

When you're really short on space or want a sleek design, consider a wall-mounted sink. These attach to the wall with hangers or angle brackets. You can find very low-priced options or custom pieces that look more like art than something you should spit into. Some have integrated faucets, while others are made as stand-alone units with the faucet mounted on the wall above.

Wall-mounted

SINK MATERIALS

FIBERGLASS
Light and affordable but prone to scratching. Choose a higher-end variety for best results.

ENAMELED STEEL
Light and affordable but chips easily.

VITREOUS CHINA
Most often found in white, but other colors can be ordered. Made from kiln-fired clay, it's easy to clean, requires no special care, and is affordable and hard to damage.

STONE
Its weight can require additional support. This porous material needs to be resealed once a year.

CONCRETE
Usually integral sinks with concrete counter-tops, these can be easy to clean and maintain as long as they are sealed regularly.

GLASS
Shows everything, so you'll need to wipe it with a cloth after each use. Usually made thick for durability and with tempered glass so it won't shatter. Blown or colored glass can be expensive.

METAL
Bronze and copper will patina with age. Abrasive cleaners will scratch them.

FAUCETS

The heavier and more expensive the faucet, the higher quality and longer lasting it will be. Choose one with either solid brass or ceramic disk workings that promises to resist stains and scratches and to be leak-proof. Manufacturers often make sink faucets and tub and shower faucets in the same designs and finishes for a coordinated look.

Centerset

◢ SINK FAUCETS ◣

Your choices will be limited by the holes in your sink and countertop if you're not changing those too. Otherwise, you can choose among centerset, single-lever, widespread, and wall-mounted styles.

Centersets combine a spout and handles in one molded piece. They are the most affordable choice—you can get them for under $100 but will pay between $100 and $200 for a well-made model. They can need either one or two holes in the countertop for the water supply pipes. If your counter has two holes, you can still buy a replacement with one connection if the base is wide enough to hide the unused holes.

A single-lever faucet should be used for universal design bathrooms. There are no hot and cold handles, just one that sits on top of the faucet and can be twisted to change the temperature of the water. They also cost between $100 and $200.

Widespread

Widespread faucets come in three pieces: one spout and two handles. Most vintage replicas are widespread. This option will cost about twice the amount of a centerset faucet.

Wall-mounted faucets are usually installed above vessel or wall-mounted sinks and can have either one or two levers for hot and cold water. The designs can range from long and skinny faucets that provide a strong stream of water to ones from which the water

Single-lever

spills slowly over a wide edge. Don't install them too far over the sink or you'll get a lot of splashes. These can be several hundred dollars or more depending on the design.

TUB FAUCETS

Tub faucets can be freestanding, wall mounted, or deck mounted. Freestanding types are used for claw-foot or soaking tubs. The pipes come out of the ground or the wall nearest the tub and are exposed.

You may need to special-order a faucet if you're using an antique tub, as the predrilled holes were made to fit sizes that are no longer standard.

Jetted and deck-mounted tubs use concealed units in which only the handles and spouts are exposed. They can be either on the edge of the tub or on the wall next to it.

Tub and shower combinations use one system that includes the faucet, hot and cold levers (or a single lever), and a showerhead. The tub faucet is connected to the showerhead with a diverter. The diverter can be in the wall, which means the valve that shuts off the water to the faucet and pushes it up into the showerhead is on or near the control handles. Or the diverter can be its own unit mounted on the wall between the showerhead and the faucet. You can also buy a handheld faucet attachment, which makes it easier to wash children or your own hair if you're taking a bath.

Be sure the tub and shower faucet you buy includes a pressure-balancing valve, which automatically adjusts the mix of hot and cold water when a sudden change in pressure occurs. All new construction requires the use of pressure-balancing fixtures.

Deck mounted

Tub and shower combination with exposed diverter

SHOWERS

There's a lot to consider when you are designing a new shower, such as deciding between a prefabricated model or building from scratch, what kind of shower head you want, whether you want multiple showerheads or wall-mounted jets, adding a built-in seat, and including a niche for soap and shampoos. Or you may decide to upgrade to a steam shower.

PREFABRICATED STALLS

These are one-piece units made out of fiberglass, reinforced acrylic, laminate, or synthetic marble. They are available in square, corner, and circular designs. Depending on the material and features, they can cost between $300 and $3,000. On the upside, these types of showers are easy to install and keep clean, and there's no way for water to seep through the walls into the structure of your house as it can if you have tiles that come loose. However, you need to have enough room to bring these monster pieces into your existing bathroom. Don't settle for one that's less than 32" across on the inside or you'll have barely enough room to move around. Prefabricated showers are usually installed in new construction when the walls aren't framed in yet. For a remodel, make sure the doorway is wide enough for you to bring the unit into the room.

CUSTOM SHOWERS

To build a shower from scratch, you can either build a mortar and masonry base or start with a prefabricated shower pan. Shower pans are available in materials such as fiberglass and cast polymer, and they come in a range of shapes and sizes. They are the best choice for do-it-yourselfers building a shower, as it takes lots of skill and practice to float a mortar base. For the shower walls, you can either choose prefabricated panels, which can include accessories like soap dishes and grab bars, or build your own walls of concrete backerboard covered with ceramic tile or stone.

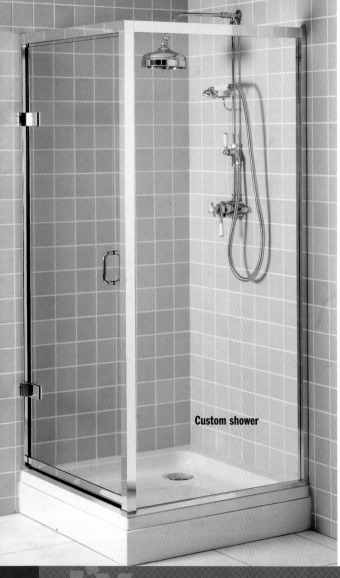

Custom shower

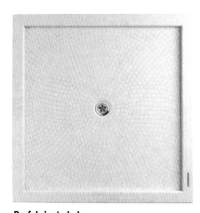

Prefabricated shower pan

SHOWERHEADS

Gone are the days when your only choice was a small showerhead with one or three water output settings. Even if you're not going to remodel your shower, consider purchasing a new showerhead for a spalike experience. Oversized sunflower showerheads release a soothing rainfall of water. Other options release a gentle flow or a steady blast of water. If you are remodeling the shower area and can reroute the water supply pipes, consider adding a second showerhead below or above the existing one, or moving the head to the center of the shower.

SPA AND STEAM SHOWERS

A spa shower is basically a standard shower with the addition of wall-mounted spray jets. You can find systems with between 3 and 10 jets to hit you in certain target areas from head to toe. Make sure you have or can add the water capacity for this kind of shower before purchasing the hardware, as one spa shower can use 50 gallons of water within 10 minutes.

A steam shower has an electric generator that heats the water and sends steam into the shower through multiple nozzles. You need a place to put the generator that's close to the shower (different models have different requirements for how many feet away) and where it can be both hardwired to the electrical system and connected to the water supply. Some require a dedicated 240-volt electrical circuit, which you may have to add. You may also need an extra water heater. A steam generator that you add to a custom-built shower costs around $1,000. Self-contained units can be bought for around $8,000 to $10,000.

For both options, make sure that you have a heavy-duty shower fan and that the shower walls are completely waterproofed. Otherwise all that steam and strong water sprays may damage the structure of your bathroom.

DOORS

Tempered glass and fiberglass doors are generally installed in aluminum framing that lines the bottom and sides of the shower. You can also choose a frameless shower door system, but they're more expensive. Consider ordering glass that is colored or textured so it's harder to see through. Take into account how much space you have around the shower before deciding on how the door will open. Sliding and pivoting doors are good options for small spaces.

Spa shower

BATHTUBS

The tub is often the centerpiece of the bathroom, whether it's recessed into an alcove, dropped into a tub deck, or freestanding in the middle of the floor. If you have a standard fiberglass or acrylic tub in white or almond, you may not realize the wide world of styles currently on the market. There's no need to settle for the ordinary when you can have a truly unique design, a jetted tub, a claw-foot tub, or a soaking tub to make your bathroom remodel even more special.

Soaking tub

Recessed tub

RECESSED TUBS

A recessed tub fits between two sidewalls and along a back wall, and it has a finished front apron. Corner models are finished on one side and one end so that they can wedge between two walls. Both options are usually tub-shower combinations. This kind of tub is usually made of enameled steel and can cost as little as $200. Enameled steel is lightweight and noisy, and it can chip fairly easily. Acrylic or plastic tubs come in many colors and cost about $400. Enameled cast iron is a long-lasting choice and is warmer than enameled steel, but it's so heavy that you'll have a hard time getting it into place and you may need structural reinforcement if your floor isn't strong enough to support it. Cast-iron tubs can cost between $300 and $900 depending on the design.

SOAKING TUBS

Soaking tubs have similar qualities to recessed and freestanding varieties, but they're deeper. You can find them in almost any material, from acrylic to cast-iron enamel to copper and even wood. They can sit against the wall or in the middle of the floor, and some are big enough to hold two people. The only downside to a soaking tub is its weight. The tub can hold about 500 pounds of water, and some of them are made of materials that can weigh 300 pounds. Most people have to reinforce their floor before installing one. You'll also want to make sure your water heater is large enough to handle the additional output.

JETTED TUBS

Basically deeper tubs with jets, these can be free-standing, built into a tub deck, or dropped into the ground. It may be tempting to buy one that the whole family can fit into at once, but make sure you don't choose something that's too big for your space. You can test them out by sitting in dry floor models. Remember that it may look small in the showroom but will seem much larger once you get it home. You can choose fewer jets that produce a more powerful surge of water, or many jets that hit you with less force. Water jets are better for a more vigorous massage. Air jets are more delicate, but they're noisier and lose heat more quickly. Whichever kind you choose, be sure to flush the tub twice monthly to prevent bacterial buildup.

The motor can be hidden in a tub deck, but if you have a claw-foot tub, you can either route the tube through the wall or floor to an adjoining room or build a small plumbing cabinet in the bathroom to house the motor and water supply pipes for the faucet. Expect to pay between $1,000 and $5,000, depending on the size, shape, and features.

Jetted tub

CLAW-FOOT TUBS

It's possible to find a reconditioned antique, but many companies manufacture replicas with modern bells and whistles like air jets. A slipper tub is a claw-foot with an elongated back for more support while you're bathing. Claw-foots usually have freestanding faucets that come out of the floor or the wall, so be sure you can extend your plumbing to the right spot before you buy. They are available in many materials, finishes, and colors, making them ideal for period, Victorian, modern, and country bathrooms. The feet can be found in chrome, polished brass, nickel, and more. Claw-foots can cost between $1,400 and $3,000 or more, depending on finish and features.

TIPS | DIY Network Home Improvement

Bathtub Restoration

Perhaps your remodeling plans don't call for a new tub but the one you have has seen better days. If the enamel has been chipped, you can find products to fill in small holes. If you hate the color but it's otherwise sound, look into having it recoated with porcelain (see page 124). It doesn't cost much and will last about 5 years. For a more long-term solution, have a refacing company fit an acrylic tub liner over your existing tub (see pages 128-129).

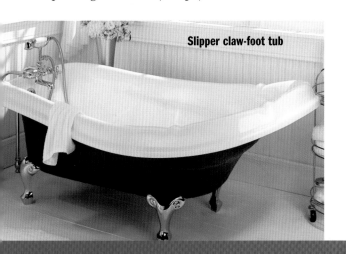

Slipper claw-foot tub

Toilets & BIDETS

Just like bathtubs, these once innocuous bathroom fixtures are experiencing a renaissance of styles and options. From ultra-low-flow to pressure-assisted, electronic, and wall-mounted, there is sure to be a toilet that will meet and exceed your requirements. Part of the reason for the variety of options is that federal law now mandates that all new toilets use no more than 1.6 gallons of water per flush. Traditional gravity-flush systems don't work as well with this limited amount of water, making pressure-assisted models more popular.

Bidet

One-piece pressure-assisted toilet

◢ TOILETS ◣

Two-piece models come with a bowl and a separate tank but do not include the seat cover. Standard, gravity-fed models in basic white can cost less than $100. Manufacturers make two-piece models in different designs with round and elongated bowls, and they look right in traditional, period, and country bathrooms.

A one-piece toilet can cost between $300 and $800, depending on the color, style, and features. It's easier to clean because it doesn't have a joint, and it generally comes with a toilet seat. One-piece toilets lend themselves to sleek and modern bathrooms.

Gravity-fed toilets are quieter but less efficient than pressure-assisted models. Vacuum-assisted toilets cost more than pressure-assisted and have less flushing power. Be sure you have at least 25 pounds per square inch of water pressure before buying a pressure-assisted toilet. Gravity toilets with a flush valve of 3 or more inches work better than those with 2-inch valves.

If you're buying a new toilet for an older home, make sure it will fit before you buy. The offset—the distance between the wall and the center of the drain hole—should be 12 inches for a new model to fit. Elongated toilet bowls extend 29 to 31 inches from the wall, while rounded bowls extend 25 to 28 inches, making them preferable for small spaces.

BIDETS

More common in Japan and Europe but gaining popularity in America is the bidet, meant to offer additional hygiene. To add a bidet, you'll need to extend your hot- and cold-water supply lines to a spot near the toilet. The water is sprayed horizontally into the air or vertically from the center of the bowl. It drains through either the floor or the wall. Bidets are offered in a variety of colors and designs to match the toilet they will probably be sitting next to.

LIGHTING

Be sure that all bathroom light fixtures are UL approved and suitable for damp areas. Lighting fixtures placed in or within about 6 feet of the shower or tub must be rated for wet use.

BULBS
Fluorescents provide better light than they used to and are also energy efficient, but halogens are still the best choice for lighting around the mirror because they reflect skin tones most accurately.

AMBIENT
Light that comes from a ceiling fixture, window, or skylight that bathes the entire room in a soft glow.

TASK
Light that's needed where grooming or reading is done. Spotlights, track lighting, recessed lighting, small overhead fixtures, and wall sconces can all provide task lighting.

RECESSED
Provides task or accent lighting. Good for small spaces or low ceilings where a large fixture would get in the way.

ACCENT
Consider shining a spotlight, track light, or recessed light onto an interesting architectural feature or piece of art in the bathroom. If you have a freestanding tub in the middle of the room, this would be a good way to draw more attention to it. Be sure the light won't shine directly into your eyes when you're in the tub.

WALL-MOUNTED
Wall sconces on each side of a mirror that's 36 inches wide or smaller will minimize shadows cast on your face.

STORAGE

A basic storage rule is to always keep objects near where you plan to use them, which will help you find and return things more easily. If you've decided to replace your vanity cabinets with a pedestal or wall-mounted sink during your remodel, you may now be realizing that you have to find someplace else for all of your toiletries and towels to go. Before putting a new storage system in place, go through everything you keep in the bathroom and throw away all those little hotel soaps and bottles of shampoo and cream you haven't used in years. Once you've purged, buy only as much storage equipment as you need, which will hopefully lower the number of things that migrate to the bathroom.

Glass shelf with towel rack

Most items are stored on the walls with hooks and pegs, in cabinets that either sit on the floor or hang from the wall, or in freestanding pieces of furniture that often combine shelves and small drawers. If you don't have much floor space, you will need to utilize the walls. Small wood or glass shelves placed near the sink are perfect for items you use every day, and they will provide a more open look than a solid cabinet hanging on the wall.

Wall niches are also good solutions for limited storage space (see photo, next page). Find two wall studs that don't have any electrical or plumbing between them, then simply cut out the drywall. Frame the opening with pieces of wood and new pieces of drywall to cover the four sides and back. Tape the seams, apply joint compound, prime, paint, and you have an integrated storage niche that's very accessible yet out of the way.

Hook

To keep things looking neat on open shelves or even behind glass doors, look for coordinated boxes and bins to hold small items that can start to look cluttered. They will also help keep like things together. For example, if you store first-aid materials in the bathroom, gather all the boxes of bandages, tubes of ointment, and wraps and put them in one box so you'll be able to find them all quickly when the time comes.

HOOKS AND PEGS

Good replacements for long towel bars when you don't have the wall space. Also helpful for hanging robes, shower caps, and clothes that need a place to dry.

SHELVES

Hang three short and narrow shelves near the sink for small bottles and toiletries. You can also find shelves made for corners, although sometimes they are large enough to hold only one item per shelf. Put any items that might roll off the shelves in little boxes.

BASKETS

You can store towels and toiletries in matching baskets on the floor, on shelves, on top of cabinets, and pretty much anywhere else. If you find yourself constantly picking up discarded clothes from the bathroom floor, consider putting a tall basket with a lid in the bathroom as an alternate hamper to keep things looking tidy.

PLASTIC BINS

A great solution for keeping bath toys off the floor and out of sight. Wipe the inside occasionally so that mold doesn't grow in the water that drips off the toys.

FURNITURE

Freestanding cabinets, dressers, and armoires give the bathroom some style in addition to providing large amounts of storage space. If you buy something that wasn't made to go in a bathroom, make sure it has a moisture-proof finish. Wood dressers and armoires can be finished with marine-grade polyurethane to protect them from water damage.

Furniture

Wall niches

Baskets

Finishing TOUCHES

It's the little details that can make or break the way your bathroom comes across. Now that you've made all the major purchases and installations, it's time to have fun with the accessories. Look beyond the basic necessities. You can add a personal touch to your bathroom by always having a small bouquet of fresh flowers on the vanity or a signature scent like jasmine or lavender drifting out from a scented candle.

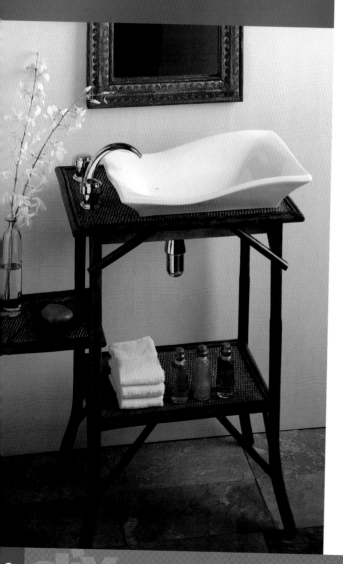

TOWELS

Turn your old, thin towels into rags and splurge on new towels for your remodeled space. Plush, thick towels not only feel luxurious but look better hanging on the wall. Pick one or two colors that go with your new walls and floor. Roll up some extra hand towels and arrange them in a basket on the floor or on a shelf in a cabinet.

RUGS

These should be color coordinated with your towels and provide a thick cushioning for your feet. Have one in front of the vanity and another one that can be washed more frequently in front of the tub or shower. If you have a large bathroom, consider putting a long rug in the middle of the floor as a visual accent.

WINDOW COVERINGS

Choose a window covering that works with the style of the room. For example, shutters or blinds for contemporary bathrooms and sheer curtains or vinyl pull-down shades for period or retro bathrooms. Make sure whatever you choose gives you the right amount of privacy and will be easy to keep clean.

Heated towel rack

TOWEL BARS AND HOOKS

Buy high-quality bars and hooks made of solid brass finished with chrome, nickel, or brass plating. If you have the wall space, put one or more towel racks near the tub and shower. Use hooks where space is limited or for hand towels near the sink. Hooks and short towel racks can also be installed on the backs of doors to hang towels and other personal items. Both should be installed about 48 inches off the floor and never over a heat vent, receptacle, or light switch. For kids, hang them closer to 36 inches. Double towel racks have an elegant look, as do heated towel racks like those found in fine hotels. They look right at home in period bathrooms.

SHOWER CURTAINS AND RINGS

There are a wide variety of prints and colors available in shower curtains. You can buy a clear liner and use it alone or cover it with a printed curtain made of plastic or fabric. Kids enjoy shower curtains with integral pockets to hold toys and shampoos. Install a curved shower rod to give you more space to move around. Shower rings can be found in different colored plastics or in period styles with small round balls on top that roll instead of scratch along the top of the shower rod.

MIRRORS

There should be at least one mirror over the vanity. Add a second one on another wall to enlarge the space. If children will be using the room, hang a mirror low enough for them to see. Attach a pull-out mirror to the wall above the vanity that you can use while applying makeup.

SOAP DISHES AND TOOTHBRUSH HOLDERS

Choose elegant glass or porcelain soap dishes and toothbrush holders for adult bathrooms. In kids' bathrooms, use plastic or acrylic so they won't shatter if dropped on the floor.

Plastic accessories for kids

Wall-mounted soap dish

diy
network

2

Projects

Now that you've decided what to do, let's talk about how to do it! The following bathroom projects are some of my favorites, and each of the homeowners did a great job getting their hands dirty in the process.

There were times in several of these projects where the homeowner's opted to call in a professional. You're saving so much money by doing most of the work yourself—don't hesitate to get help with the areas you're unsure of.

If I could only stress one thing, it would be safety first! Get out your gear: work gloves, eye protection, ear protection, long sleeves for demolition and work with insulation, and a dust mask or respirator are the bare minimum for most projects.

The first step is out with the old. If the idea of ripping out a dividing wall or shattering your old tiles or cast iron tub to pieces scares you, don't worry. It can be very therapeutic! Once the old bathroom (or the parts of the bathroom you are changing) have found their way to the recycling center or trash bin, it's time to bring in the new.

This chapter will lead you through a variety of projects, from simple updates and repairs, to period remodels, to the ultimate high tech bathroom. You can mix and match the information to fit your bathroom project, and you'll learn some new skills that you can use not only to fix up your bathroom, but your entire house!

Good luck and don't forget to have fun!

ART DECO

The bathroom in this 1940s home was last renovated in the 1970s and was literally falling apart. After waiting several years to start their remodel, the homeowners spent just a few weeks creating this black and white art deco-style bathroom, which fits beautifully with the vintage look in the rest of the house.

BEFORE: Besides having no discernable style, the old bathroom was missing tiles and had leak problems.

AFTER: High-end materials helped turn an eyesore into one of the best rooms in the house.

◄ PROJECT SUMMARY ►

By doing most of the work themselves, the homeowners were able to spend their $20,000 budget on high-quality period fixtures and accessories, a new toilet and sinks with art deco details, a white Carrera marble countertop, custom-made black cabinets, and a unique art glass panel that separates the tub from the toilet. They saved money on tile by choosing machine-made white subway ceramic field tiles and porcelain black and white pinwheel tiles for the floor instead of hand-made tiles or stone. The homeowners also saved by keeping the original bathtub, which was in good condition.

But this wasn't just a cosmetic makeover. Leaks behind the shower walls meant that the entire tub surround needed to be torn down to the studs. Changing the configuration of the shower fixtures and adding a second sink required some plumbing work behind the walls. But by not cutting corners, the homeowners now have a stylish, functional, and leak-free bathroom that will last for years to come.

The glass panel visually opens up the space in an otherwise cramped and isolated spot.

AFTER: From the art deco light fixtures to the crystal cabinet knobs, the sink area is high on style.

BEFORE: The beige laminate countertop had to go.

You Will Need

Reciprocating saw	Metal channel
Glass panel	Hacksaw
¾" plywood	Laser level plumb bob
Adhesive	Drill
1¼" screws	Silicone caulk

INSTALLING THE ART GLASS PARTITION WALL

1 The homeowners removed the original tiled partition wall in pieces by cutting from the outside edge toward the back wall with a reciprocating saw (photo A). Once you get close to the back wall, stop cutting and simply push or kick the wall down, being careful not to rip a hole in the ceiling.

2 A short knee wall was then built to support the new glass panel. Make a knee wall out of two ¾-inch pieces of plywood screwed together and set it flush against the side of the tub (photo B). Screw the knee wall into the cleats underneath the tub to support it. Then cut pieces of concrete backerboard that will cover the front, back, and sides of the plywood and screw those on with 1¼-inch screws. Check for level and plumb.

3 Use a hacksaw to cut pieces of metal channel in the shape of the glass panel. Screw these pieces to the knee wall, back wall, and ceiling.

4 Carefully slide the glass panel into the metal channel without chipping the edges of the glass (photo C).

5 Once you know it fits, remove the glass panel while you finish the rest of the renovation. When it's installed at the end, seal the edges with a bead of silicone caulk.

TIPS | DIY Network
Home Improvement

Carrying Glass
Use a heavy-duty suction cup to carry large pieces of glass. Look for them at your local tool rental store.

You Will Need

Safety glasses	Solder
Work gloves	Copper pipe and fittings
Adjustable wrench	Gas torch
Wire brush	Spacer blocks
Teflon tape	Flux
Impulse nailer	Cleats
Backerboards (green-treated plywood)	Concrete backerboard

◢◢ REPLUMBING THE SHOWER ◣◣

The shower needed to be replumbed in order to use the new fixtures the homeowners purchased (see the sidebar at right for more information). There was a panel in the adjacent room that opened up to the supply pipes for the shower, so this was relatively easy to do. If you don't have a similar access panel, you should be able to do the plumbing work from the wall that opens up into the shower.

1 In order to install copper pipe that will connect to the new fixtures, you first need to know where those fixtures will be. There are no rules about this. Just hold each piece up and decide where it looks best to you. Cut pieces of ¾-inch green-treated plywood and install them between

the wall studs—you'll attach the new fixtures to these pieces of backerboard. Nail cleats to the studs, then nail each piece of plywood to the cleats with an impulse nailer (photo A). Once the boards are in place, screw them in for added strength.

2 Snap a chalk line on the backerboard to mark the center and then drill holes through each piece using a hole saw. Make sure each fixture fits in its hole before moving on.

UPDATING TUB AND SHOWER FIXTURES

Ever turn on the sink in the kitchen and hear a yelp from the person showering in the bathroom? Then you must live in an older home with original plumbing. When this bathroom was remodeled, the homeowners bought scald-free tub and shower valves (mandated by most states in new construction), which will prevent inconvenience and possible injury from dramatic water temperaturefluctuations.

However, this new fixture required that the water supply pipes meet up horizontally (as shown above) rather than vertically, the way they do in most old homes. So this shower needed to be replumbed in order to accommodate the new tub and shower fixtures.

Before starting any plumbing project, always shut off the water. Since the work may take a while, it's best if the water is shut off only in the room you're working on and not to the entire house. If there are no shutoff valves in your bathroom, install them before you work on the rest of the plumbing (see pages 168-169 for more information).

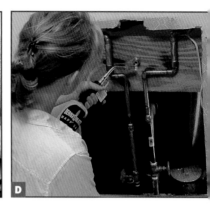

3 The new supply lines need to meet up with the backs of the new fixtures. But if you construct the new lines before the wall is finished and then try to attach the fixtures, they may not reach the new pipes. To mimic the finished wall, put spacer blocks the same thickness as the tiles and concrete board between each fixture and the backerboard, then screw the fixtures back on (photo B). Now you'll know how far to extend the pipes.

4 On a flat, fireproof work-surface, construct a series of copper pipes and fittings that will bring the existing pipes to the new fixtures (photo C).

Use a wire brush to clean the ends of the fittings and then apply flux (or solder paste) with a brush to the outside of the pipe and the inside of the fittings. Solder the fittings to the pipe.

5 Working from the access panel, attach the new supply lines to the valves. Wrap the threads of the valves clockwise with Teflon tape. Then screw on the fittings and tighten them with an adjustable wrench. Attach 90-degree elbow fittings to both sides and solder them into place (photo D).

TILING THE SHOWER

The homeowners decided on white machine-made subway tiles for the shower walls, capped with a black chair rail. A row of green glass tiles acts as a border that continues around the entire room.

Before they could get started on the tiling, the walls needed to be closed in. Insulation with an R value of 11 was set between the studs. Then the concrete board was added, screwed to the studs with porcelain-coated screws that won't rust. A bead of silicone caulk fills the gap between the board and the existing tub.

Take measurements of the tiles and the walls and decide on the layout of the tiles so you don't end up with a small sliver on one end. Since the glass tiles will go around the room, make sure their height on the wall will work everywhere before setting them in the shower.

You Will Need

Silicone caulk	Pencil
Tiles	Wet saw
Spacers	Mastic
360-degree laser level	³⁄₁₆" V-notch trowel
Tape measure	

A

1 Use a wet saw to cut two chair rail tiles at a 45-degree angle (photo A). They will form the picture frame corner that will border the shower. Tilting the saw base to 45 degrees gives the perfect cut.

2 Use a laser level to mark a line for laying the tiles. Spread double-duty mastic with a ³⁄₁₆-inch V-notch trowel from the laser line down the side of the tub. Start tiling in the corner, applying each tile with a slight twisting motion (photo B). Use spacers to ensure even spacing.

B

3 Before you place the field tiles, determine where the accent tile will go. Add up the height of the new floor, vanity, countertop, and courses of subway tile over the countertop to figure out where to place the accent tile. Find that spot around the room by using a 360-degree laser level (photo C). Mark the laser line so you'll know how many courses of subway tiles you'll need between the accent tiles and the chair rail border.

C

4 To set the field tiles, use a V-notch trowel to apply an even coat of mastic about three courses down. You have about five to 10 minutes to set the tiles, so don't apply too much adhesive. Again, set the tiles with a slight twisting motion (photo D). The glass tiles are set in the same way.

TIPS | DIY Network Home Improvement

Cutting Tile
Use a wet saw with a diamond blade to cut ceramic and glass tile. The diamond blade is more precise than a score-and-snap tile cutter, and it will give you a professional-looking cut every time. Buy one for around $100, or rent one for about $40 per day. Replace the blade when it stops making clean cuts.

D

You Will Need

Heat gun	Circular saw with carbide blade
Hand scraper	Jigsaw with carbide blade
Mask and gloves	Thinset mortar
Knee pads	Drill
Slam scraper	Mixing paddle
Screwdriver	¼" x ¼" square-notch trowel
Tape measure	1½" galvanized deck screws
½" concrete board	

FLOOR DEMOLITION AND UNDERLAYMENT

In preparation for the new floor, the old flooring needed to be removed. Tiling over it was not an option because some pieces were missing and there were spots where the floor felt squishy underfoot, indicating that a stronger subfloor was needed. If you tile over a bouncy floor, you risk getting cracks in your new tile and grout. Concrete board provides a strong and stable subfloor as well as better adhesion for the new tiles.

1 To remove an old vinyl floor, use a heat gun and scraper (photo A). Be sure to wear a mask so you don't inhale the dust. Don't overheat the tile. You just want to warm up the glue underneath so that it loosens enough for you to pry up the vinyl with the scraper.

2 Once you remove the old flooring, use a slam scraper to get rid of any leftover glue (photo B). You can rent one for about $15 per day. They work quickly and efficiently, but be careful with the sharp blade. If the subfloor looks stained, test it by poking the area with a screwdriver. If the screwdriver doesn't go through the wood, the floor is stable. If the wood is rotted, you need to replace that section before putting down the concrete board.

3 Take careful measurements of the entire floor. Then cut pieces of ½-inch-thick concrete board to fit the room. Use a circular saw with a carbide blade for the straight cuts and a jigsaw with a carbide blade to cut out holes or notches (photo C).

D

4 Dry-fit the concrete board in the room. When you have every piece ready, remove them and mix a batch of thinset mortar using a drill with a mixing paddle until it is creamy.

5 Apply the thinset on the subfloor with a ¼-by-¼-inch square notch trowel. Lay the board working from the far corner of the room out toward the door. Then go back and fasten the boards to the floor with 1½-inch galvanized deck screws (photo D). Drive them in every 6 to 8 inches.

You Will Need

Tiles	Thinset mortar
Tape measure	Plastic bucket
3⁄16" V-notch trowel	Hand mixer trowel
Grout	

SETTING FLOOR TILES

The homeowners chose a pinwheel mosaic pattern for the floor, which was often used during the art deco era. The tiles are made of porcelain and come in 12-inch sheets on mesh backing. In the center of the room, the pinwheel pattern is accented with black center tiles, creating a ruglike effect between the sinks and the bathtub. The edges of the floor were finished with a glossy black tile cove base.

1 Measure between the tub and the cabinets to decide where the tile "rug" will be (photo A). Instead of centering it in the middle of the room, the homeowners centered it in front of the tub, since that's the focal point of this room.

2 Spread thinset mortar on the floor using a 3⁄16-inch V-notch trowel. Then set the tile sheets with an even, gentle pressure (photo B). Setting the rest of the floor will go pretty quickly. In this project, the homeowners decided to grout the shower, walls, and floor all at once when all the tiles had been set.

A

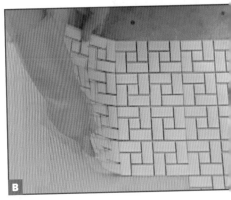

B

You Will Need

Tape measure	Clamps
Safety goggles	3" cabinet screws
Drill	Shims
Level	Faucet
Pencil	Putty knife
Hole saw	Silicone caulk

B

C

INSTALLING CABINETS AND SINKS

1 Holes need to be cut in the back of the cabinets so the two supply lines and one drain line can go through. First measure to be sure the cabinet will sit flush against the wall without hitting a windowsill or door frame. If you need to place the cabinet an inch or so away from the wall, use fill stock to cover the gap. Once you have found your spot, measure from the cabinet edge to the center of the pipe, then up from the floor to the center of the pipe. Mark those spots on the back of the cabinets.

2 Use a hole saw to make the cuts. Start cutting outside the cabinet and finish from the inside (photo A) so that if it splinters, the rough cut will be against the wall. Then fit thecabinet over the pipes.

3 Once all the cabinets are in place, clamp them together at the face frames. Drill pilot holes and then screw the cabinets together using screws provided with the cabinets (photo B). Check for level and use shims under the toe-kick if you need to. In the back, screw the cabinets into wall studs using 3-inch cabinet screws. Now the countertop is ready to install (see page 125).

4 Install the faucets on the sinks before attaching the sinks to the cabinet. For instructions on installing a typical three-piece faucet, see pages 164-165. Once the faucet is in place, apply a ring of silicone sealant under the rim of the sink and set the sink in place on the countertop (photo C). Scrape off any excess putty and run a bead of clear silicone caulk around the perimeter.

You Will Need

- Safety glasses
- Knee pads
- Tile
- 360-degree laser level
- Mastic
- Heavyweight rosin paper
- Painter's tape
- Pencil
- ³⁄₁₆" V-notch trowel
- Wet saw
- Silicone caulk

SETTING THE TILE RAIL AND COVE BASE

The glass tiles in the shower were carried over to the other walls in the room. Before they were set in the shower walls, measurements were taken to be sure they would fall in the right spot all the way across the room. Before you start tiling, protect your new floor with heavyweight rosin paper. Commonly used under hardwood floors, it is a great and inexpensive protector.

1 Start by establishing a reference line around the room using a 360-degree laser level (photo A). Make a series of reference marks for the top and bottom of the tiles so you'll know where to spread the mastic.

2 Use a ³⁄₁₆-inch V-notch trowel to apply the mastic adhesive to the wall. Mastic is better than thinset mortar when you're setting wall tiles because it grips the tile right away so it won't slip down the wall before the mastic dries. A laser level is particularly handy for tiling, as a pencil line would be covered by the mastic.

3 Cove base tile is installed around the perimeter of the room. Back-butter these tiles by applying mastic with a V-notch trowel and wiggling them into place on the wall (photo B). Once all the wall tiles are set, apply grout followed by a bead of silicone caulk where the tiles meet the wall. The caulk will prevent moisture from seeping in behind the tiles.

INSTALLING A MARBLE COUNTERTOP

The homeowners chose a white Carrera marble countertop for their art deco bathroom. It's not an inexpensive choice at $40 per square foot, but it adds a touch of elegance that a tile or solid-surface countertop would not. When you buy a slab of stone for a bathroom countertop, the installers will leave in the cutouts for the sinks until the countertop is set in place. This adds stability to the marble when it's moved from the manufacturer to your home. Once the counter is in place, the cutouts are removed with a 5-inch diamond blade. To avoid having the heavy cutouts slam down on your new cabinets and floors, the installers use double suction cups and a 5-foot aluminum pole to keep the cut piece from falling through the hole.

After the countertop is installed, a bead of silicone caulk is applied to seal it in place.

COTTAGE

The downstairs powder room in this adorable lakeside summer cottage didn't go with the rest of the house at all. The walls had been textured and faux painted in a rust color, while the boxy cabinet and sink were too big for the small space. This bathroom also needed a lighter color scheme and a more open, cottage-style design.

AFTER: Adding watery colors and a little architectural detail made a huge difference.

BEFORE: The powder room didn't exactly say "lakeside cottage."

◀ PROJECT SUMMARY ▶

The existing cabinet, sink, and toilet were removed. Inside the cabinet, Amy found some old and rusty plumbing that wouldn't work with the pedestal sink the homeowner wanted to install. So a professional plumber was called in to cut out the existing pipes under the floor and reroute them behind the wall. That way, the water supply and drain pipes would stick out of the new wall right where they needed to for the pedestal sink. The new matching sink and toilet look great, and the pedestal makes the small bath feel much larger.

To add some cottage flavor, the homeowner chose bead board for the lower walls. She covered up the faux-painted walls with a coat of bright cream paint, and the existing flooring was covered with a synthetic version of a sisal rug, which will withstand the rigors of bathroom use. New lighting fixtures and a cream-framed mirror with a ledge provided the icing on the cake.

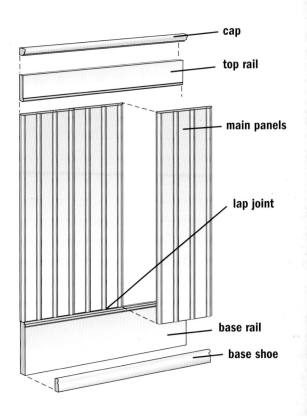

cap

top rail

main panels

lap joint

base rail

base shoe

You Will Need

- Tape measure
- Sliding compound miter saw
- Jigsaw
- Construction adhesive
- Level
- Pin nailer
- MDF bead board

◢ INSTALLING BEAD BOARD ◣

Classic bead board is made out of solid wood and tends to expand and contract, which may cause gaps between the slats in a moist area like a bathroom. The homeowner chose an MDF (medium-density fiberboard) bead board instead, which won't have that problem. MDF bead board is also very easy to put together. It's made with lap joints (photo A) that fit together so you can mix and match the different pieces. In this bathroom, the main panels sit on a base rail piece with a shoe and are finished off on top with a rail and separate cap piece.

1 Start by installing the base rail piece and build up from there. Remove any existing baseboard and shoe, take measurements of the walls, and cut the new base rail pieces to length. Use a sliding compound miter saw to make 45-degree cuts where the corners will meet up.

A

TIPS | DIY Network Home Improvement

The Order of Work

The bead board should be installed before the new flooring. When you put the flooring in, you will butt it up against the bottom of the base rail. The shoe will then be placed on top of the flooring and up against the bottom of the base rail, hiding any gaps and providing a clean, finished look.

2 When installing bead board, make sure all the slats are plumb. To do so, check that the base rail pieces are level. Set the base rail on the highest point on the floor. As you go around the room, you will have gaps in the areas of the floor that are lower, but the base shoe should cover the irregularities (photo B). To adhere the bottom rail to the wall, apply a heavy bead of construction adhesive along the length of the board and press the board to the wall.

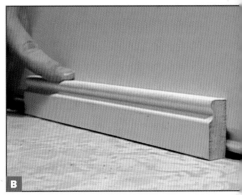

B

SMOOTHING OUT A TEXTURED WALL

This bathroom had a textured wall finish that didn't match the smooth walls in the rest of the house. Before repainting the bathroom, the homeowner smoothed the walls by applying a thin layer of watered down joint compound. Sold premixed in tubs, joint compound is a little too thick to use for skim coating. But if you add some water and a little liquid dish soap (which takes any bubbles out of the joint compound) and mix with a paddle until creamy, it works like a dream. With a 10-inch taping knife, spread a thin layer of the modified joint compound over the walls. Don't pile it on. You want just enough to fill in the pits and depressions in the wall. Once it's dry, sand down any rough patches with fine sandpaper. Then you're ready to prime and paint.

3 Once the base rail pieces have been installed, it's time to set the main bead board pieces. Apply adhesive to the back of the bead board and, starting in the corner, set the lap joint into the track of the base rail. Check that the board is plumb, and make adjustments if necessary. It's important that the first course be absolutely straight. Once each piece is in place, secure them all with a pin nailer (photo C). Nail into the narrow profile of the bead board to hide the nail heads as much as possible.

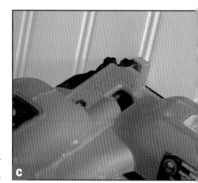

4 After all the bead board is up, the top rail can be installed (photo D). Repeat the process: adhesive on the back, press firmly in place, and secure with nails. Don't install the cap until the upper wall is finished and painted.

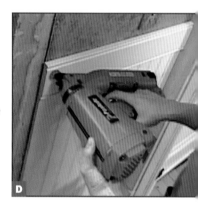

TIPS | DIY Network Home Improvement

Irregular Cuts
Most of the bead board cuts are pretty simple and can be made with a miter saw, but for small cuts around the window, you will need to use a jigsaw to get the proper profile.

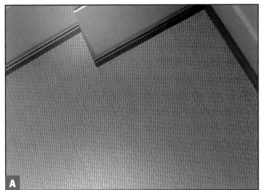

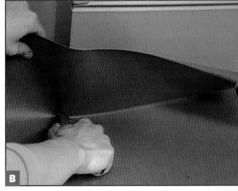

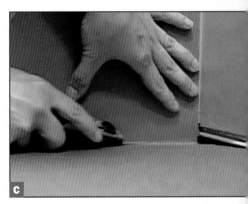

You Will Need

Vinyl rug	Painter's tape
Rosin paper	Spray adhesive
Utility knife	Double-stick tape

▰ INSTALLING WOVEN VINYL FLOORING ▰

The homeowner chose mock-sisal flooring for her new cottage bathroom. True sisal rugs are actually made of woven grass, which wouldn't hold up well in a bathroom. This flooring mimics the color and texture of sisal but is actually made of water-resistant woven vinyl (photo A). Since this bathroom is so small, the homeowner was able to buy a large rug and cut it down to size rather than pay for a professional installation.

1 Make a template of the bathroom floor with rosin paper. You'll use this template to cut the flooring out in the right shape. Lay one edge flush with the wall and roll it out across the room. At the opposite end, let some excess paper lap up the side of the wall and cut that piece off the roll. Carefully jab a utility knife into the corner and slice upward (photo B). This makes a relief cut that allows the paper to lie flush against the wall.

2 Fold the paper back, crease it along the wall, and cut along the edge with a utility knife (photo C). Continue this process until the paper lies perfectly flat around the perimeter of the space. Work slowly and carefully around the doorframe. If you make mistakes, just use tape to patch things up.

TIPS | DIY Network
Home Improvement

Utility Knives
Use a new blade and change blades often or you will rip the paper instead of slicing it.

3 The paper will probably not be wide enough to span the bathroom floor, so attach another layer to the first using a spray adhesive to complete the template (tape can shift, causing problems when you cut the flooring). After spraying on a couple of passes of adhesive (photo D), hold the pieces apart for a few seconds to let the adhesive tack up, then press the edges together.

4 In another room, roll out the rug finished side up on a piece of plywood or other hard surface that's safe to cut on. Place the template on top. Tape the edges of the template to the rug every few feet so it won't shift (photo E).

5 Use a utility knife to cut out the rug along the edges of the template (photo F). This rug has a thick vinyl backer, so you will have to apply good pressure. Work slowly and make sure you change the blades as soon as they start to get dull.

6 Once you have finished the cutout, position the rug onto the bathroom floor. If your bathroom is very small, you can just use double-stick tape to attach it to the existing flooring rather than glue it down. Then attach the shoe to the base rail, which will cover up any rough edges and help hold the flooring in place (photo G).

TIPS | DIY Network
Home Improvement

A Clean Paint Job
It's a good idea to paint baseboard and shoe molding before nailing them to the wall. You'll save yourself the trouble of having to tape off the wall and protect the new flooring, and you'll be able to paint or prime the backs of the pieces as well so that wood boring insects don't find it down the line. Countersink the nails, cover the holes with putty, and dab a little paint over each hole for a seamless finish.

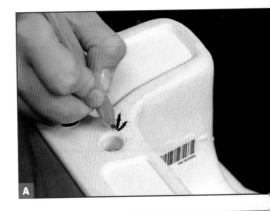

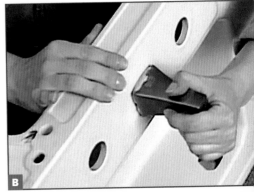

You Will Need

Pedestal sink	Wrench
Safety goggles	Carpenter's pencil
Power drill	Level

◢ INSTALLING THE PEDESTAL SINK ◣

Installing a pedestal sink is fairly easy, but it does need to be properly supported. A porcelain pedestal holds up the sink, and the sink is attached to the wall. The bolts that hold the sink in place should to be screwed into a stud inside the wall. Use a stud finder to see if you have one where you want to mount the sink. If not, you'll need to install a piece of 1-by-2 lumber in the wall before you put up the bead board.

1 First mark where the mounting holes on the back of the sink will meet the wall (photo A). Drill pilot holes to match in the wall. The support bolts are threaded on both ends. Put the acorn nut on the machine-threaded end and use it to drive the lag screws into the wall.

2 Install the faucet assembly before attaching the sink to the wall (photo B), as it is much easier to reach the back now than it will be later. (For information on installing a faucet, see pages 164-165.)

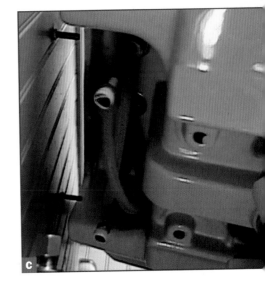

3 Pull the acorn nuts off the mounting screws and fit the sink over the holes, placing it on the pedestal (photo C, from below). The acorn nuts go back on with a washer and get tightened with a wrench.

Kids' BATHROOM

For a family with two young children and more to come, devoting one bathroom in the house to their needs makes perfect sense. The homeowners chose an under-the-sea theme for a bright, welcoming, and tranquil space that their kids will be able to use safely for years to come.

BEFORE: The antique-car themed bathroom just wasn't doing it for the kids.

AFTER: This bright new space made with their needs in mind is a room they never want to leave.

PROJECT SUMMARY

The pea-green tile, antique car wallpaper, and original toilet were removed. The homeowners transformed the existing vanity by cutting down one side for a lower sink, painting the doors and drawers with a decorative technique that looks like drops of water, and adding a new solid-surface countertop with integrated sinks. Walls were brightened with white ceramic tile and random accents of aquamarine glass tiles. Watery-blue wallpaper continues the theme above the wall tiles, and new PVC tiles that look like a shimmering ocean make for safe and durable flooring. Low storage cubbies will keep things organized, and a kid-size porcelain toilet means no more plastic potty training toilets for this family. Topped off with new mirrors at two different heights, track lighting with remote control sensor, gleaming faucets, and a host of safety features, the kids will be begging for bathtime!

BEFORE: The old sink was too high for the kids to reach unassisted.

AFTER: Now there's a low sink and a high one so kids of all ages can brush their teeth without having to stand on a stool.

BEFORE: The kids had a hard time using the closet because the doorknob was out of their reach.

AFTER: Individual cubbies at kid-height make it easy to hang up robes and put away shoes.

You Will Need

Speed square	Screwdriver	Paintbrush
Japanese pull saw	Circular saw	Foam brush
Hammer and nails	Random orbital sander	Denatured alcohol
Rubber mallet	Sanding sponge	Paint
Level	Primer	Polyurethane sealant

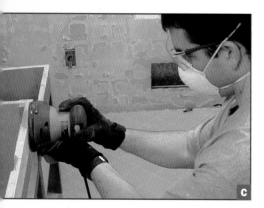

CREATING A KID-SIZE VANITY

Instead of buying an expensive custom-built cabinet, the home-owners decided to save some money by cutting down one side of their existing wood cabinet to a kid-friendly height. The vanity is topped with a solid-surface countertop with two integrated sinks. Now the kids are able to reach the lower sink without standing on a stool. To go with the water-themed design, the cabinet drawers and doors are finished with a decorative paint technique that looks like drops of water.

1 Remove the drawers and doors. In this project, the cabinet was lowered 4½ inches. Remove any drawer slides that are in the area you'll be cutting down.

2 Use a speed square to mark the stile for the new height (photo A). Then use a Japanese pull saw—a great tool for making precise cuts—to cut out the existing stile (photo B). This piece is then tapped into place with a rubber mallet on a lower stile.

3 Mark where the sides of the cabinet will be cut and check for level. Use a circular saw to cut the sides from the front toward the walls. Stop before you reach the wall and finish the cut with the Japanese pull saw. You'll need to add a new support brace to the back of the cabinet between the two sides to hold up the new countertop. Cut a piece of scrap lumber for this purpose and screw it in place.

4 Sand the outer surfaces of the cabinet, doors, and drawers with a random orbital sander fitted with a fine-grit pad (photo C). For the grooves, use a sanding sponge.

5 Give everything a coat of acrylic (water-based) primer. In this project, a decorative paint technique was used that looks like there are beads of water on the surface, which is what happens when denatured alcohol mixes with acrylic paint.

6 Mix together a small amount of acrylic paint and water to a fairly thin consistency. Use a foam brush to apply a small amount to the cabinet (photo D, previous page). Paint small sections at a time that you can finish before the paint dries, as the next step works only on wet paint.

7 Dip a small brush into a cup of denatured alcohol and drop or flick the alcohol onto the wet paint in whatever pattern you like (photo E).

8 Once everything is dry, apply a coat of polyurethane sealant to protect the painted wood surface from bathroom moisture and splashing children.

You Will Need

Hole saw	Wrench
Silicone	Tape measure
Sawhorses	Marker
Painter's tape	

INSTALLING THE SINK AND COUNTERTOP

1 Set the countertop on sawhorses for stability. Measure and mark the center of the sink (photo A), then measure and mark half way between the back lip of the sink bowl and the back edge of the countertop.

2 Where the two lines intersect, use a hole saw to drill a hole for the faucet supply lines (photo B). Pieces of painter's tape will help prevent you from damaging the countertop with the hole saw.

3 Place the faucet on the countertop and feed the supply lines and bolt through the hole. From underneath, install the retaining washer and tighten the nut.

4 Dry-fit the countertop on the cabinet base and check for level. Then tip the counter up and apply silicone all along the edges of the cabinet (photo C). Press the countertop into place.

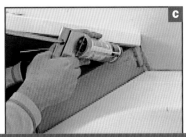

You Will Need

Mounting hardware	Drill with ½" spade bit
Screwdriver	Hammer
Tape measure	Screwdriver
Pencil	

▰ INSTALLING TRACK LIGHTING ▰

The track lights were put on a motion sensor so that when the kids come in to use the bathroom in the middle of the night, they don't need to worry about reaching the light switch.

1 Attach the mounting bracket to the ceiling (photo A) and snap the track into the bracket.

2 Measure out from the wall to make sure both sides of the track are on equal distance from the wall.

3 Mark the support holes with a pencil. Drill holes on the marks with a ½-inch spade bit (photo B).

4 Install screw anchors into the holes, then swing the track into position, tap the anchors into place with a hammer, and tighten the screws.

5 Slide and snap the lights onto the track and position them so that light hits in all the right areas (photo C).

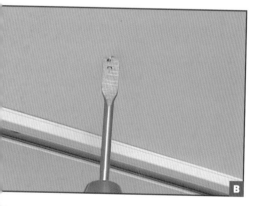

You Will Need

Wall tile	Wet saw	Sponge
Laser level	Safety gloves and glasses	Rubber gloves
³⁄16-inch V-notch trowel	Grout	Mastic
Scraper	Float	Drill with paddle attachment

▰ RANDOM-PATTERN WALL TILE ▰

Easy to clean, white ceramic wall tiles were chosen for the bathtub surround and walls of this kid-friendly bathroom. To add a touch of color and whimsy, randomly selected tiles were left off and filled in with a group of four green glass tiles. Glass tiles are installed the same way as ceramic. White ceramic chair rail tiles running along the top will finish it off.

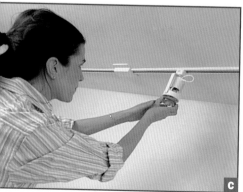

1 Once you've determined your design, use a laser level to mark the location of the lowest full tile piece around the bathtub, which is usually about 2 inches above the tub lip.

2 Nail a batten board to the wall at the mark (photo A) to support the tiles so they don't slide down the wall before the mastic dries.

3 Measure and mark the center of the wall and use that as a starting point for the tile pattern. Set a vertical laser on that line to make sure your tiles don't go off course as you make your way up the wall.

4 Dry-fit the tiles to determine where the pattern will end at the corner of the walls, and make sure you don't end up with tile slivers on either side.

5 Use a ³⁄₁₆-inch V-notch trowel at a 45-degree angle to spread the mastic on the wall. From the center line, start placing tiles along the batten board and tile up from there.

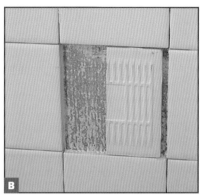

6 When you get to a spot where your accent tiles will go, skip it and continue laying the rest of the row. Then scrape away the mastic in that area and press a half piece of tile smooth side down in the spot (photo B). This tile piece will hold up the tile above it until it sets. Later, when you're ready to set the glass tile insets, this piece will pop right out with a screwdriver because the smooth side won't adhere as well to the wall.

7 To make cuts for the corners, determine how much needs to be cut off, then set the fence to the right spot on a wet saw and run the tiles through (photo C).

8 Back-butter the chair rail pieces with mastic (photo D) and press them into place.

9 Once the mastic has set, remove the half-piece tile spacers. Back-butter the glass accent tiles (photo E) and press them into place. Set each one with a slight twist.

TIPS | DIY Network
Home Improvement

Setting Uneven Tile

These glass art tiles are not all the same height, so Amy picked each one off the mesh backing and grouped them into batches of four that were approximately the same size. When placed, each set of four was even.

10 When the walls are all tiled and the thinset has cured, it's time to grout. Using a drill with a paddle attachment, mix up a batch of grout, adding more or less water until the mix is the consistency of peanut butter. Let it sit, or slake, for 10 minutes before use.

11 Apply the grout with a rubber grout float. Draw the float across the tiles at a 45-degree angle (photo F). Your fingers are better tools to get grout around the glass accent tiles.

12 With a wet sponge, wipe away the excess grout (photo G), drawing the sponge across the tiles at a 45-degree angle.

KIDS' ART PROJECT

Mom had a great idea to take the kids to a local ceramic art store where they could paint their own tiles. She used the same white tiles that were purchased for the bathroom walls, but after the painted tiles were baked, the white tiles turned a bit dark. They no longer seemed to work as a tile backsplash behind the sink, as they were originally intended. So Amy suggested framing the tiles and hanging them on the wall. This way, the color difference wouldn't be so obvious and the framed tiles could be moved around in the bathroom or to another room later on.

Amy laid out the tiles, measured them, and cut a thin piece of luan wood to set them on. She applied a bead of construction adhesive on the backs of the tiles and adhered them to the wood. Then she used a miter saw to cut some leftover window casing and made a frame around the tiles. The casing was glued to the wood base with more construction adhesive and clamped together until dry.

You Will Need

- Utility knife
- Scissors
- Flat edge
- Laser level
- Natural sponge
- Long shallow tub for soaking wallpaper

HANGING WALLPAPER

1 Measure the width of the wallpaper roll and mark that measurement on the wall out from a corner.

2 Line up a vertical laser level line on the mark. That will be the edge of the first sheet of wallpaper.

3 Measure the height of the wall space to be papered. Add 4 inches to that length so you will have a 2-inch overlap at the top and bottom. Cut a piece of wallpaper to size. Use this first piece as a template to cut several more to length.

4 Roll up an individual sheet and soak it in water, making sure all the air bubbles have escaped. Take the roll out of the water (photo A) and fold the top of the wet strip two-thirds of the way down so paste rests on paste. Let it relax for 2 to 3 minutes while you prepare more strips.

5 Start at the top of the wall and work down, leaving 2 inches of overhang at the top and bottom. Spread the wallpaper out with your hand first and then smooth the air bubbles out with a flat edge (photo B).

6 Trim the excess off by running a utility knife against the straight edge. At the top of the wall tiles, run a utility knife where the wallpaper meets the tile (photo C). Wipe away the paste on the wall left over from the excess wallpaper with a damp natural sponge before it dries.

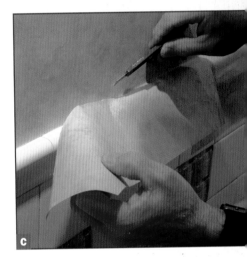

7 To wallpaper around a window, hang the wallpaper as usual and then cut around the window with a utility knife, following the gap between the drywall and the window casing. This works only if the window molding has been removed first.

TIPS | DIY Network Home Improvement

Buying Wallpaper

Always check that each roll of wallpaper you buy is from the same lot number (the numbers should be printed on the labels). Otherwise, the rolls may have been printed on different presses and a slight color change may be obvious once the wallpaper is put up.

You Will Need

¼" birch underlayment	Skimcoat	Putty knife	Tile adhesive trowel
Circular saw	Paddle mixer	Gloves	Cloth
Pneumatic stapler with 1⅜" quarter-round staples	Bucket	Eye protection	Utility knife
Knee pads	Mask	Straightedge
Clamps	Flat trowel	PVC tile adhesive	100 lb. roller (rented)

◀ LAYING PVC FLOOR TILE ▶

Slip-resistant, waterproof flooring is the perfect choice for a kids' bathroom. PVC tiles that look like shimmering water make this under-the-sea-themed bathroom even more unique. To install any thin resilient tile, a smooth subfloor is key. This subfloor was bumpy and had lots of joint lines. So Amy and the homeowner got to work putting down a smooth birch underlayment with as few seams as possible.

1 Measure the floor to figure out how to cut the underlayment and end up with as few seams as possible. Cut the birch pieces to size with a circular saw.

2 Use a pneumatic stapler to attach the underlayment to the subfloor (photo A) every 6 inches in a grid pattern.

3 A thin layer of cement skimcoat is then used to fill in any seams and indentations in the wood. Combine the skimcoat with water in a bucket and blend until smooth. Apply a thin layer to the underlayment with a flat trowel (photo B). After 15 minutes, use a putty knife to scrape off any high spots.

4 Mark the center of the room with a chalk line. Mix the PVC adhesive according to the manufacturer's instructions. The adhesive is toxic, so protect yourself with rubber gloves and eye goggles, and open windows for ventilation.

5 Spread adhesive with the trowel that comes with the PVC flooring (photo C). Apply adhesive only on as much of the floor as you can tile before it starts to dry.

6 Place the tiles on the floor (photo D) and push gently. If any adhesive seeps up through the seams, quickly wipe it away with a soft cloth. To make cuts, simply use a utility knife and a straightedge on a solid surface.

7 Rent a 100-pound roller from a home center and roll it over the entire surface once the adhesive is dry.

TIPS | DIY Network Home Improvement

Wood Underlayment
Birch was chosen because it's a clear, light wood. If you used a darker wood like luan under resilient floor tiles, the color might bleed through the adhesive and into the tiles, causing them to discolor.

You Will Need

- Melamine panels
- Circular or trim saw
- Construction adhesive
- Nail gun with 1½" finish nails
- Drill
- ½" screws
- Shelf pins
- Stop collar for drill bit

◢ BUILDING STORAGE CUBBIES ◤

To help keep towels, robes, slippers, and tub toys organized, Amy and the homeowners built four small "lockers" made of white melamine. This product can be found in home improvement centers. Melamine is laminate-coated MDF, so it's easy to work with, inexpensive, and prefinished, so no painting is necessary.

1 Cut the pieces to size using a circular or trim saw. Assemble the base by gluing pieces to the walls and side of the cabinet with construction adhesive. Once the pieces are up, nail them into place using a nail gun with 1½-inch finish nails (photo A).

2 To finish the base, add a front piece and a support piece in the middle for strength. Then set a flat piece on top of the supports to create a platform. The platform is attached with construction adhesive and finish nails.

3 Now cut pieces for the top, bottom, and vertical sides of the cubbies and attach these pieces with countersunk ½-inch screws. Instead of making fixed shelves, drill shallow holes in the sides and use shelf pins that can be pulled out and placed higher or lower as needed. Use a stop collar on the drill bit to keep from drilling all the way through the wood (photo B).

KID-SIZE ACCESSORIES AND SAFETY FEATURES

Did you know you can buy a kid-size toilet? It's perfect for those potty-training years. For this growing family, it made sense to incorporate one into their kids' bathroom, especially since there is another bathroom in the house for adults to use. Toilets are relatively inexpensive and definitely easy to install and remove, so when the kids outgrow this one, it will be no problem to replace it with a standard fixture.

In addition to the kid-size toilet and lowered sink, a host of safety features for kids were incorporated in this bathroom. A swinging arm keeps the toilet lid down when not in use so small children don't fall in and don't throw any of their toys in either. An oversized anti-slip rubber mat, protective cover over the water spout, and suction grip handle on the tub's edge for getting in and out keep bath time injury-free. And a splash guard that's held by suction cups on each side of the tub keeps water where it belongs, lessening a child's chance of slipping on a wet floor while getting out the tub.

STYLE UPDATE

Sometimes you don't need a complete overhaul to change the look of your bathroom. In this case, the homeowners needed to do a few repairs but otherwise liked the way their bathroom functioned. With just a few days of work the bathroom looked like a completely new space, which shows what a major impact color can have on a room.

BEFORE: Outdated wallpaper wasn't doing anything for this bathroom.

AFTER: Strong color and accessories make it look like a totally new space.

◢ PROJECT SUMMARY ◣

The 1980's wallpaper was removed, and the walls were painted a deep burgundy. The existing vanity got a simple face-lift with new hardware and a gleaming new faucet. The old toilet had some cracks, so it was replaced with a new model. Some of the grout in the tiles around the bathtub had worn away but the surrounding tiles were in good shape, so the homeowner's carefully removed it and applied new grout (see page 157). Since this master bathroom has a lot of space and the closets are nearby, the homeowners decided to install a built-in ironing center, which hooks up to existing electrical lines. It's covered with an oak cabinet door stained to match the oak vanity, so when the unit is closed, it looks like just another cabinet.

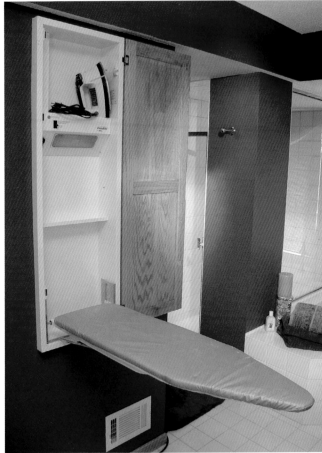

This elegant new faucet really makes a statement.

A hide-away ironing board isn't difficult to install and saves space in other rooms of the house.

You Will Need

Tape measure	Jab saw
Level	Reciprocating saw
Cardboard	Screwdriver
Pencil	

INSTALLING THE IRONING CENTER

This ironing center is made to fit between two wall studs. The studs in this wall weren't 16 inches apart, as they should be, so one stud had to be moved over to accommodate the unit. The wall the homeowners chose to install it on already had wiring running to a receptacle, so it was easy to tap into the existing line.

1 Find the middle of the wall where the ironing center will go and mark it with a pencil. Use a level to draw a straight, vertical line down the center of the wall.

2 Make a template of the ironing center out of cardboard. Line up the center of the template with the center mark on the wall and draw a pencil line around it (photo A).

3 With a jab saw, cut out a square of drywall within the outline of the template (photo B) that is large enough for you to reach your arm in and carefully feel around for any obstructions. Cut very slowly so you can stop yourself before accidentally cutting into a wire or pipe.

4 Once you've determined there are no obstructions behind the wall, you can remove the rest of it. Finish cutting around the template with a jab saw.

5 In this case, there was a stud in the way, so Amy cut it out with a reciprocating saw, moved it over 16 inches from the stud to the left, and screwed it into place. Now the ironing center could be attached to studs on each side, as it was meant to be.

TIPS | DIY Network Home Improvement

Screwing into Drywall

When screwing into drywall, don't set the screw too deep. Ideally, you don't want to break the paper on the surface of the drywall. A slight dimple is perfect.

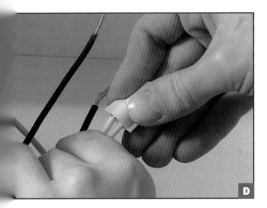

6 Slide the iron cabinet into place (photo C on previous page) and secure it to the wall studs with screws.

7 Turn off power at the breaker panel. Then tie the ironing center into the existing electrical wiring in the wall by stripping back the supply wire. Use wire nuts to connect it to the leads on the cabinet (photo D). Then hide the electrical work by screwing in the cover plate provided in the ironing cabinet.

You Will Need

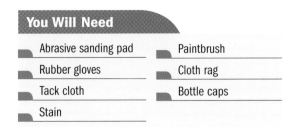

Abrasive sanding pad	Paintbrush
Rubber gloves	Cloth rag
Tack cloth	Bottle caps
Stain	

STAINING THE CABINET DOOR

The homeowner ordered an oak cabinet face for the ironing center. Once he found the right color of wood stain to match the existing vanity, he and Amy got to work.

1 Lightly sand the door to remove any splinters or rough patches (photo A). Use an abrasive pad instead of sandpaper so you don't inadvertently change the profile of the wood grooves. Always sand with the grain of the wood. Wipe away the sanding dust with a soft tack cloth.

2 Wearing rubber gloves, apply the stain with a paintbrush, again with the grain of the wood (photo B). Keep the application as even as possible.

3 Once the surface is covered, remove the excess stain with a cloth rag (photo C). Don't let the stain sit too long before removing the excess, as the longer it sits, the darker the stain will be.

4 Flip the door over onto a few bottle caps so you can stain the back while the front is drying.

Period RESTORATION

The master bathroom in this 1910 Tudor-style home was the victim of a 1970s remodel, complete with a blue bathtub and sink, carpeting, and odd lighting. Luckily, the fixtures worked and they had no water damage, so all the homeowners needed to worry about was how they wanted the new room to look. They decided to bring the bathroom back to its original glory by restoring it with period fixtures that have modern function.

BEFORE: No one could bear to spend any time in front of this bathroom vanity.

AFTER: The refurbished antique vanity sitting under an elegant mirror and sconces competes with a gorgeous clawfoot tub for attention.

◀ PROJECT SUMMARY ▶

This busy couple with three young children enjoy working on their home, but they simply didn't have time to complete a major bathroom remodel all on their own. So they hired professionals to reroute plumbing and electrical lines, hook up the radiant electrical in-floor heat system, pour a solid subfloor, and restore the window. But they saved about $5,000 by doing their own demolition and much of the installation. They prepared the sub-floor for the concrete underlayment, installed cultured marble wainscoting, tiled the floor, hooked up a jetted claw-foot tub, retrofitted antique furniture to act as a vanity and makeup table, and installed a pull-chain toilet. They also took care of finishing touches such as crown molding, new wall sconces and a chandelier, a hanging shower rod, new window molding, and framed mirrors. With Amy by their side, they got a lot of work done in a relatively short period. And the results of their hard work are spectacular.

AFTER: Period fixtures, a classic color scheme, and tasteful accessories turned this bathroom into a show-stopper.

BEFORE: The old bathroom had a turquoise toilet and sink, and beige carpeting. What more do you want?

You Will Need

Small bucket	Circular saw
Gloves	Pry bar
Eye protection	Hammer
Tape measure	Plywood
Pencil	8-penny ring shanks
Chalk line	

◢◢ REPAIRING THE SUBFLOOR ◣◣

After gutting most of the bathroom, the homeowners hired a plumber to remove the old wet wall (a wet wall is any wall that contains plumbing). The plumber moved the water supply lines and the drain to the middle of the wall, which is where it needed to be for the new claw-foot tub. Once the old tub was removed, it was clear that the subfloor was sagging in one corner. This is a common problem in older homes. But the claw-foot tub needed to be level and shims would have nowhere to hide. Plus, the plan included using a liquid self-leveling floor, so it was important to get the firmest base for that as possible. The homeowners went about replacing the sunken section of the subfloor. The floor had been cut up many times over the years, so they needed to create a straight line where the new plywood would meet the old.

1 Measure out from the wall in two locations to an area of the subfloor that is sound (photo A) and snap a chalk line.

2 With a circular saw, cut out the old plywood. Then use a pry bar to lift out the old piece (photo B).

3 Cut the new plywood so the seam rests on a joist (photo C). You can leave the debris that is under the subfloor there, as it doesn't hurt anything and will act as a sound barrier.

4 Secure the plywood to the joists with 8-penny ring shanks (photo D). The ring shanks help keep the subfloor from shifting or squeaking .

You Will Need

Circular saw	Plastic lath sheeting
Scrap lumber	Radiant floor heat system
Impulse nailer	Latex primer
Duct tape	Self-leveling concrete
Staple gun	Electric drill with mixing paddle
Foam tape	Large float

POURING A SELF-LEVELING CONCRETE FLOOR

To create a perfectly level floor, it was decided that a self-leveling concrete underlayment should be poured. Since the homeowners were short on time and didn't have the proper tools for this job, they hired a professional to pour the floor. But first they did a series of things to prepare the subfloor.

1 Cut seams between the sheets of plywood subfloor with a circular saw (photo A). This creates a gap so the sheets can expand and contract under the concrete, which helps prevent the tiles from cracking later on.

2 Nail in a piece of scrap lumber across the door opening to act as a dam for the self-leveling underlayment (photo B). Once the concrete has hardened, the scrap piece can be removed.

3 Use duct tape to seal the seams between the sheets of plywood (photo C). This will keep the liquid underlayment from leaking through before it sets up. Also fold pieces of 2-inch duct tape into an L shape to seal the gap between the floor and the walls.

4 Staple foam tape around the perimeter of the room (photo D). This will allow for expansion between the subfloor and the wall and will also create a thermal barrier to increase the efficiency of the in-floor heating system.

5 Attach plastic lath sheeting to the plywood subfloor with staples (photo E). The lath will give the finished floor more stability.

6 Then the electric radiant heat system was installed over the plastic lath sheeting and before the self-leveling underlayment.

7 The installer sprayed a latex primer over the entire subfloor (photo F). This will wet the plywood and help the gypsum concrete adhere to the floor. Using a drill with a special mixing bit, gypsum was blended with water and sand until it was the consistency of a runny milkshake. The mixture was then poured over the floor in batches.

8 A large float was used to smooth out the surface (photo G), and then the liquid was allowed to self-level. After four hours the floor was dry and ready to walk on.

You Will Need

Utility knife	Thinset mortar	Wet saw
Tape measure	Mixer	Tile nipper
Pencil	Drill	Rosin paper
Chalk line	¼" square-notch trowel	
Bucket	Margin trowel	

TILING THE FLOOR

The homeowners chose black and white pinwheel tiles that came on mesh sheets for easier installation. A rectangle of black inlay tiles that wrap around the room breaks up the pattern and adds interest. Always dry-fit tiles before you start laying them so you're sure that the layout will work and that you won't end up with irregular pieces at the edges. Once the pattern is set, center the design in the room.

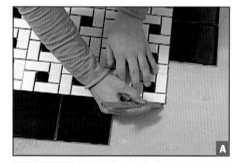

1 Mark the corners with a pencil (photo A) and then pick all the tiles up off the floor. Snap chalk lines from corner to corner to make a box for the field tile.

2 Mix the thinset mortar to a peanut butter consistency and allow it to slake (rest) for about 10 minutes. Spread it on the concrete floor using a ¼-inch square-notch trowel (photo B, previous page) and then begin to set the tiles. A wet saw can be used to cut the ceramic field tiles. For cuts that need to go around tight areas such as a radiator, use a tile nipper.

3 Back-butter the inlay tiles using a margin trowel (photo C) and set them in place. Once all the tiles are set, protect the new floor by covering it with rosin paper for the remainder of the remodel. Later, the floor will be grouted and sealed.

WINDOW RESTORATION

The old rope-and-pulley window in the bathroom had seen better days. The upper sash was painted shut and the lower sash would not stay open on its own. The window was also quite drafty in winter. The homeowners could have replaced the window, but since this was a period restoration, they decided to restore the one they had. This is not a do-it-yourself project, so a window restoration expert was called in. The following steps will give you an idea of how this process works.

1 Because of the age of the house, it was possible that the window trim was covered with lead paint. As a precaution, the trim was sprayed with water before it was dismantled, which reduced the amount of dust created.

2 The trim and stop were removed. If the old screws are stripped, pieces can be carefully removed with a pry bar (photo A). Next the lower sash and middle piece (called the parting stop) were removed. The old rope was cut and the upper sash pulled out.

3 After the old pulleys were taken out, the old iron weights were removed from the weight pockets. These empty pockets were stuffed with fiberglass insulation to improve energy efficiency (photo B).

4 Next a shim was added to the blind stop to create the correct spacing for the new jamb liner. The access panels and retainer clips that secure the jamb liners were stapled in (photo C), and then the jamb liners snapped into place. A sash stop was also installed.

6 The installer cut the old windows down to fit the new jamb liners. A groove was routed in the sides to receive the pin that connects the window to the jamb liner. Another groove was cut out for the weather-stripping, which was tapped into place (photo D).

7 Finally, the window was taken back to the bathroom and put in place. The refurbished window is now energy efficient, and it opens and closes like a dream.

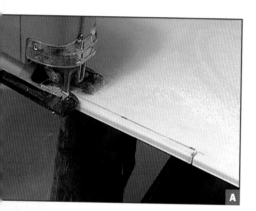

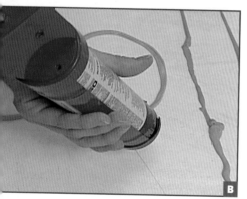

You Will Need

Measuring tape	Level
Jigsaw	Gloves and safety glasses
Construction adhesive	T-square

INSTALLING CULTURED MARBLE WAINSCOTING

The homeowners wanted to use marble somewhere in their bathroom renovation. The idea of using marble slabs as wainscoting around the walls appealed to them, but the cost and weight of real marble was prohibitive. Then they found out about cultured marble, which is much lighter, easier to work with, and less expensive. Cultured marble is a mixture of fiberglass resin and crushed limestone. The materials are mixed in the factory and poured into an open mold. The color and veining of marble are then added and the mold is baked to a hard, waterproof surface. Finished, polished pieces have the look and feel of real stone.

1 Dry-fit the first piece. Make sure it is plumb and level and then mark that spot on the wall.

2 To cut around molding or a window, first mark the height on the cultured marble panel. Measure how far it extends past the obstacle. Using a T-square, transfer these measurements to the panel and cut it with a jigsaw (photo A). Cut slowly and carefully, as the panels can crack.

3 Apply a generous amount of construction adhesive to the back of each panel (photo B) and press them into place on the wall.

You Will Need

- Hammer
- PVC flexible hose
- PVC primer and glue
- Circular saw
- Plumber's putty
- Screwdriver
- Star wrench

INSTALLING AN AIR-JET CLAW-FOOT TUB

Several new fixtures with period style were used in this remodel, including a claw-foot tub with nickel-plated feet. While it looks like an antique, this soaking tub actually has air holes along the bottom edge for soothing champagne bubbles. The motor unit for the tub isn't difficult to install. The trick is finding the right place to put it. If you're building a raised tub deck, the unit can fit underneath. But in this bathroom it had nowhere to hide. Since the bathroom is on the second floor, the motor unit was installed in the attic right above the bathroom.

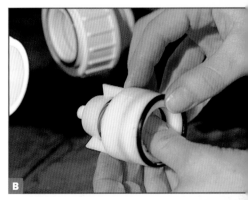

1 Cut access holes in the drywall near the floor and ceiling. To keep out debris, temporarily tape the end of the PVC hose that will pump air into the tub and then thread it through the wall and into the attic (photo A).

2 Attach a coupler to the hose using PVC primer and glue. Next, insert a check valve, which allows air to travel in only one direction so that air and water can't flow back into the pump (photo B). Then attach the hose to the pump.

3 Before putting the tub in place, make an access panel for the plumbing that needs to be done later for the faucet (an access panel was needed because this bathroom has wainscotting that the homeowner's didn't want to disturb for future repairs). From the open wall in the bathroom, drill four pilot holes through the drywall into the adjacent room (photo C). These holes will show you were to cut on the other side of the wall. Then use a circular saw to cut out the lath and plaster in the adjacent room.

4 A few more things need to be done before the plumber can make the final connection. Add plumber's putty to the tub's drain gasket and fit the gasket and the waste line in place. Use a star wrench to tighten the drain gasket (photo D). Then wipe away the excess putty and screw on the strainer cap.

5 Slip the overflow onto the drain tube and lock it in place with the retainer. Attach the drain lever to the plunger rod with a cotter pin, slide on the overflow cap (photo E), and screw it into place. Then tighten the compression fittings on the drain, and the tub is ready to be hooked up to the main supply and drain lines.

You Will Need

Tape measure	Drill with stop collar	Hole saw
Pencil	Torpedo level	Drill

INSTALLING THE FAUCET ON THE CLAW-FOOT TUB

1 Determine the height at which the faucet will be mounted to the wall. Put a plywood backer in the wall between the studs so the faucet has something sturdy to attach to.

2 Drill a pilot hole from the access wall in the adjacent bedroom (photo A). Get as close to the stud as you can while allowing room for the plumbing. This is the hot-water side of the faucet.

3 Measure the distance between the hot and cold inlets on the faucet (photo B) and transfer that measurement to the wall. Make sure the holes will be level.

4 Drill another pilot hole for the cold side of the faucet, this time from the bathroom instead of the access panel. Put a stop collar on the drill (photo C) to keep it from going too deep and hitting the plumbing behind the wall.

5 Use a hole saw over the two pilot holes to cut through the cultured marble wainscoting (photo D).

6 Slide the faucet into place (photo E) and tighten the bolts.

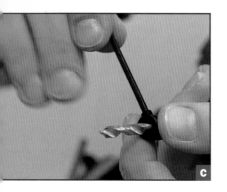

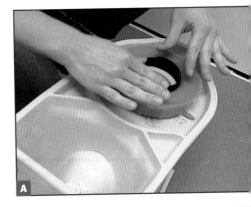

You Will Need

Wax ring	Tubing cutter
Anchors and screws	Strap wrench
Screwdriver	

INSTALLING THE PULL-CHAIN TOILET

Toilets used to have an elevated tank with a hanging pull chain to flush. Back then, the tank had to be placed up on the wall so gravity could assist in flushing the toilet. Today, toilets don't have that problem, so the tank can be right above the base. But you can still find new versions of pull-chain toilets for period restorations like this.

1 Determine the height at which the tank will be mounted. There is no right answer; just put it where it looks best to you and isn't in the way of anything else.

2 Put a new wax ring on the bottom of the toilet bowl (photo A) and set it in place. Then tighten the bolts, being careful not to crack the porcelain.

3 Screw the anchors and screws into the wall where the tank will be mounted and lift the tank into place (photo B).

4 Put the elbow on the spud and tighten it (photo C).

5 Cut the pipes running from the tank to the bowl to size with a tubing cutter. Attach the top and bottom of the pipes with compression nuts. Use a strap wrench to tighten the nuts so you don't mar the finish (photo D).

6 Determine how long you want the pull chain to hang and then attach it to the tank. Connect the water supply line.

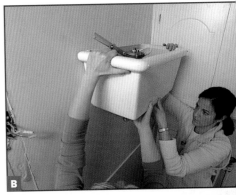

You Will Need

Rubber mallet	Anchors
Reciprocating saw	Silicone
Jigsaw	Acetone
Drill	Screwdriver

RETROFITTING AN ANTIQUE VANITY

In keeping with the period theme, the homeowners found two antique dressers that they wanted to retrofit as a vanity and makeup table for the bathroom. The dressers are topped with new custom-made quartz composite countertops, which look like real stone but won't stain and are easy to maintain in the bathroom.

1 First the pieces that are no longer needed must be removed. Take off the wooden top of the dresser by hitting the underside with a rubber mallet. With a reciprocating saw, cut out the plywood center that separated the drawers. Then saw out the center rail (photo A).

2 Lay the cabinet down on its front and measure and mark where the plumbing will come through the back. Cut out the plumbing area with a jigsaw.

3 Dry-fit the new vanity top to make sure it will work. Then flip the vanity top upside down, dry-fit the undermount sink, and mark its outline.

4 Place the sink clips and mark each one. Then remove the sink, drill holes into the new vanity top for the clip anchors, and drop the anchors into place (photo B).

5 Clean off the countertop surface with acetone. Add a bead of silicone (photo C) and then reposition the sink and install the clips (photo D).

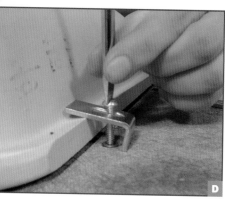

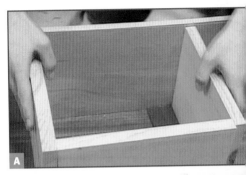

You Will Need

- Pencil
- Jigsaw
- Adhesive
- Nail gun
- Piano hinge
- Jeweler's screwdriver
- Screws

⫸ MODIFYING THE VANITY DRAWERS ⫷

Amy and the homeowners modified the cabinet drawers to make room for the sink plumbing. Then they created a tip-out drawer for storage using a piano hinge.

1 Mark the drawer for the cutout while the drawer is still in the cabinet. Then remove the drawer.

2 A box is constructed that will be attached to the inside of the drawer. That way, items in the drawer won't fall into the opening created to accommodate the plumbing. Cut 1-by-8-inch boards to create a horseshoe box (photo A). Apply an adhesive made for bonding wood to the boards.

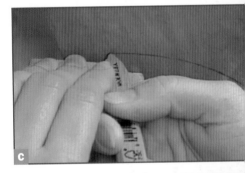

3 Line up the boards on the marks and nail through the bottom and the back. With a jigsaw, cut out the back panel for the plumbing (photo B).

4 The top drawer is no longer very large, as most of it had to be removed to accommodate the sink. But there is enough room for a few small items if the face of the drawer could hinge out rather than slide out. First you need the tip-out to clear the countertop. To do this, use a pencil held at the countertop height, tip the drawer forward, and mark (photo C). Then cut the drawer off to length.

5 Cut along the tip-out mark. Use a piece of the old drawer and attach it to the back of the tip-out (photo D).

6 Using a jeweler's screwdriver, attach the piano hinge to the drawer (photo E) and the other side to the cabinet.

INSTALLING THE SCONCES

Period light fixtures are the perfect finishing touch in this bathroom. Overhead, a crystal chandelier provides an elegant touch. But around the mirrors, wall sconces will give off soft, focused light. An electrician brought the boxes to the right spots on the walls, but the homeowner installed the fixtures herself.

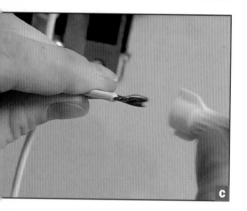

1 Whenever you're doing any wiring or electrical project, always turn off the main power at the circuit breaker first.

2 Install a universal mounting bracket to the box that will receive the fixture. Then strip the supply lines exposing half an inch of wire (photo A).

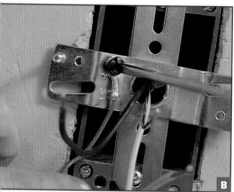

3 Attach the ground strap to the mounting bracket using the ground screw provided with the fixture (photo B). Then use a wire nut to connect the ground wire to the ground strap by inserting both wires into the nut and twisting gently.

4 Attach the common or white wire to the common supply wire with another wire nut (photo C) and then attach the hot or black supply wire to the hot wire.

5 Slide the fixture over the studs on the mounting bracket and screw on the decorative nuts (photo D). Then turn the power back on and make sure everything works.

TIPS | DIY Network Home Improvement

Wattage
Before purchasing a new light fixture, make sure it will take a bright enough bulb for your needs. It is a safety hazard to use a higher wattage bulb than the fixture recommends.

You Will Need

- Glue
- Splines
- Nail set and hammer
- Glass cutter
- Work gloves
- Clamps
- Level
- Pipe
- Tape measure
- Double-sided tape
- Sanding sponge

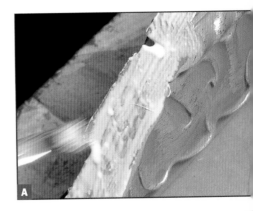

A

MAKING YOUR OWN MIRROR

Instead of buying new bathroom mirrors, the homeowners wanted to reuse the mirrors they already had. They found a company that sells just the frame, which they put together themselves. Then they simply cut the existing glass down to size and fit it in the frame.

1 Brush glue on the mitered ends of the frame (photo A) and press the pieces together. Place splines in the seams and attach them with a nail set (photo B).

2 Gently place the mirror on a sturdy work surface and measure off the area that will fit inside the new frame.

B

3 Clamp down a level that runs across your mark (photo C) and use a glass cutter to score the mirror (photo D).

4 Slide a pipe underneath the scored line and press down firmly on the short end of the mirror to break it off.

5 Use a sanding sponge to sand down the sharp edges on the cut end of the glass.

6 To hang the mirror, measure the wall to determine where the center of the mirror should be. Put a good amount of double-sided tape on the back of the mirror and stick it to the wall (photo E).

7 Put double-sided tape on the inside edges of the frame and stick the frame to the mirror.

C

E

D

SIMPLE UPDATE

After 10 years with one renter, this apartment bathroom was worn out. The classic turn-of-the-century details had lost their luster and it was time for an update. A new tenant was about to move in and the building's owner wanted to improve the bathroom with some simple cosmetic updates that would have major impact without costing major dollars.

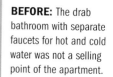

BEFORE: The drab bathroom with separate faucets for hot and cold water was not a selling point of the apartment.

AFTER: A splash of color and new fixtures add needed functionality and style.

PROJECT SUMMARY

An old-fashioned tin ceiling with matching cornice molding certainly brings back period charm. The 12-foot-high ceiling is now the focal point of the room. The toilet had been replaced a few years back, so the original pedestal sink was now replaced with a new model and faucet that matched the style of the newer toilet. All accessories such as towel racks and new lighting are period reproductions in bright chrome. Missing floor tiles were patched, the walls were given a new coat of paint in a soft two-tone blue, and a frame was built around an existing mirror for a finished look.

Tin ceiling panels give the bathroom the same kind of architectural detail that the rest of the apartment has.

A long wall was the perfect spot to hang three new towel bars.

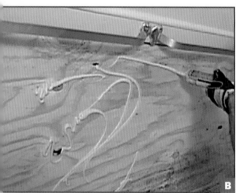

You Will Need

Circular saw	Thick work gloves	Tape measure
Tin snips	½" CDX plywood	2½" deck screws
Hammer	Construction adhesive	Drill
Steel nails	Chalk line	Sawhorses

INSTALLING A STAMPED METAL CEILING

The homeowner wanted to add some vintage charm to his bathroom and found a company that makes reproductions of old-fashioned tin ceilings. Using original stamped moldings, the company makes panels in several kinds of metal, including copper, tin, and brass. In this project, steel panels were used. The panels come with matching cornice molding for a seamless look.

1 In this bathroom, ½-inch CDX plywood was first installed on the ceiling because the existing lath and plaster were not strong enough to hold all the nails needed to secure the sheet metal. If you have a stable drywall ceiling, you can skip this step. Measure the ceiling and cut the plywood to size, making sure to use the most of each piece. If you need to rip a sheet, first put two 2-by-4 studs across your sawhorses under the plywood. Then set the blade depth of your circular saw just a bit deeper than the ½-inch material. Now there's no danger of cutting your sawhorses.

2 Find the joists in the ceiling and mark them off at the top of the wall so you will know where they are once the plywood is attached. Then take the precut plywood pieces and make a mark every 16 inches (photo A), which is how far apart the studs are in the ceiling. Use a straightedge to connect the marks. These lines will tell you where to drive screws.

3 Apply a generous amount of construction adhesive on the back of the plywood (photo B), which will give you extra insurance in case some of the screws miss a stud.

4 Lift each piece into place and use 2½-inch deck screws to secure each piece to the ceiling (photo C). Use one screw every 12 inches.

5 Just as when you're tiling a floor, it makes sense to determine how the pattern will work across the ceiling before you start to put up the pieces. For this ceiling, Amy started by finding the center on both ends of the room. She snapped a chalk line on those marks (photo D) and measured off that center line 12 inches in both directions (the panels are 24 inches across). Two more chalk lines are snapped to show the edges of the center row. This process is repeated to mark the length of the room 24 inches off the center line, giving you a grid layout for the entire ceiling.

6 Drill pilot holes at the four edges of each piece of metal so you can quickly secure them to the ceiling. With the metal pieces stacked on top of one another, drill nail holes through all the panels at once (photo E). Choose a drill bit that won't allow the head of the nail to pass through the metal sheets. When drilling the pilot holes, apply gentle pressure so you don't damage the panels or break the bit.

7 Fit the first panel into place on the ceiling and nail it up (photo F). Use steel nails to match the steel ceiling. If you use another kind of metal panel, make sure you get matching metal screws. Otherwise you could get some corrosion in a wet environment like a bathroom. The nail heads are extra deep to help prevent damaging the fragile panels when nailing.

8 The edges of the first panel are left hanging and will overlap the side panels. The panels are hung in a pattern toward the door, so you'll never see into the lap of the seam.

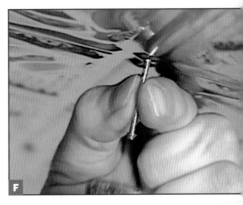

9 The cornice molding goes up in a similar fashion, each piece overlapping the next. Cut corner pieces with a miter saw for matching angles. Finish each cut with tin snips (photo G).

TIPS | DIY Network
Home Improvement

The Right Drill Bit
Use a gauge guide to determine which drill bit to use for your nail size.

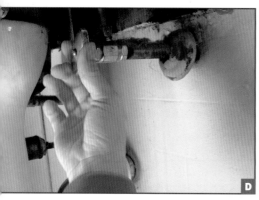

You Will Need

- Pedestal sink
- Power drill
- Pipe wrench
- Carpenter's pencil
- Teflon tape

◢ REPLACING THE PEDESTAL SINK ◣

The original pedestal sink had seen better days. It had a bit of rust, the finish had basically worn away, and there were separate hot and cold faucets with no connecting mixer, which means you couldn't get any warm water. Without too much time or money, this pedestal sink was replaced with a stylish modern version.

1 First assemble the faucets on the new pedestal sink. Apply a bead of plumber's putty at the bottom of the valve handles (photo A) and faucet. Be sure that you're putting the hot and cold water handles in the right spots and that the handles will turn in the right direction.

2 Apply plumber's putty on the bottom of the faucet bezel (photo B). Attach the faucet and two handles to the sink by tightening the nuts gently to avoid cracking the porcelain sink.

3 Attach the drain throat to the drain basket (photo C) and follow the manufacturer's instructions to complete the faucet.

TIPS | DIY Network Home Improvement

Blocking Gases
After the old sink is removed and before the new one is installed, stuff a rag into the drain line to stop any gases from backing up into the room.

4 Next attach the faucet to the water supply lines. Use Teflon tape on the tightening threads to ensure a watertight connection. Hook the water supply lines to the mixer.

5 To remove the old sink, first close the water shutoff valves (photo D). Have a bucket standing by in case they fail, and slowly remove the old water supply lines from the faucet.

6 Separate the tail of the P-trap from the wall. Now the sink is detached and you can move it out of the room.

7 Set the new pedestal sink into place and use it as a template to determine where the lag screws need to go. Mark the spots on the wall, remove the sink, and drill holes for the lag screws. Use the decorative nuts to drive the screws into the wall. Then remove the nuts, put the sink back in its spot, and hand-tighten the decorative nuts to hold the sink in place.

8 Now that the sink is attached to the wall, you may want to slide out the pedestal to work on the trap. Connect the trap and the water supply lines (photo E).

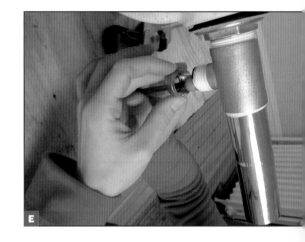

You Will Need

Tape measure	Router	Silicone
Nail gun	Screw gun	
1½" screws	Wood putty	

◢ FRAMING A MIRROR ◣

The old mirror stretching across the bathroom wall was in good shape, but it lacked any charm or character. So Amy and the homeowner decided to build a wooden frame around it to match the medicine cabinet on the opposite wall. They built the new frame in pieces and attached it to the wall around the existing mirror so as not to disturb or break it.

1 Measure the mirror to determine the length and width of the frame. Cut the wood framing pieces to the appropriate length and use a router to cut out a pocket for the mirror.

2 Nail up the sides of the frame, then nail up the top and bottom pieces (photo A).

3 Add a sill board that matches the one on the medicine cabinet. This piece will help support the weight of the mirror, so screw it into the studs instead of using nails.

4 Cover the screw holes with a false front and nail it into place (photo B). Then add back band molding pieces to the top and sides.

5 Before priming and painting, cover the nail holes with wood putty, sand them smooth, and add a bead of silicone between the mirror and the frame for stability.

SPA RETREAT

The owners of this master bathroom longed for a spalike retreat, but instead they had a dark and cramped bathroom with a huge jetted tub that hadn't worked in years. So they decided to rip out everything and start over. Now they can enjoy the fruits of their labor in a tranquil and high-end space.

BEFORE: This jetted tub took up too much space and was barely ever used.

AFTER: A slim and modern freestanding champagne-bubble tub better fits the space. The new window between the tub and shower area adds needed light.

BEFORE: A solid wall of cabinets made the room feel small.

AFTER: Slim hanging cabinets now flank an open vanity with a vessel sink.

PROJECT SUMMARY

This bathroom is split up into his and hers areas. His area includes a sink, toilet, and the shower, and her area has a sink, cabinets, and tub. To allow more light into the smaller area with the shower, a window was cut out of the dividing wall and filled with a translucent polycarbonate panel with natural reeds inside. The reeds provide privacy but still allow light to pass through. The old vanities were replaced with matching wooden stands topped with vessel sinks, which really opened up the space. Porcelain tile covers the floor and shower, and a unique tile "rug" under the tub adds warmth and texture. Two new cabinets hanging from the wall provide storage space, and a custom curved track light brightens up every corner of the room. A luxurious body-jet shower system (shown at left) with a custom glass doors and a sophisticated, freestanding champagne tub complete this spa retreat.

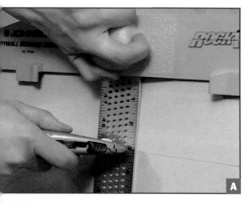

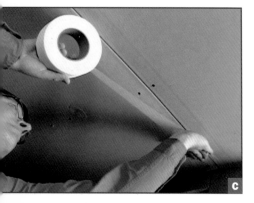

You Will Need

Straightedge	Drywall
Utility knife	Self-adhesive mesh tape
Drill and drywall screws	Putty knife

COVERING UP A POPCORN CEILING

The homeowners were never fond of the popcorn ceiling in the bathroom and had even tried to remove it years ago. So they took this opportunity to get rid of it once and for all. Removing a popcorn ceiling involves wetting it down and scraping off the popcorn, which is a messy and possibly dangerous job if there's asbestos in the ceiling. An easier path to a smooth ceiling is to cover the popcorn with new drywall.

1 Measure the ceiling to determine your cuts. Using a special drywall cutting tool (or a straightedge and utility knife), score a line across the drywall (photo A). Give the cut end a little pressure and snap the piece off.

2 Use a stud finder to locate the ceiling joists, then mark the walls a couple of inches down so you'll know where the joists are when you're placing the new drywall.

3 Along with several helpers, lift the drywall up against the ceiling and screw it into the ceiling joists (photo B).

4 Tape the seams with self-adhesive mesh tape (photo C). Then, with a putty knife, spread joint compound over the tape, pushing it into the seams to ensure a strong seal (photo D). In this case, the homeowners didn't worry about taping the edges where the ceiling meets the walls, as that would be covered with cove molding.

TIPS | DIY Network Home Improvement

Covering Up a Popcorn Ceiling

If you want a textured ceiling but don't like popcorn, try covering the existing popcorn with plaster. Use a hopper to spray the plaster onto the ceiling and then swirl it around with a large float or other flat-edged tool until it's to your liking.

You Will Need

Miter saw	Level
Right-angle driver	Speed square
Laser line	Drill
Reciprocating saw	2½" screws

▰ FRAMING THE NEW SHOWER WINDOW ▰

Showering in this bathroom used to be a bit like showering in a cave. Because the shower is in a separate room with no window, it didn't get much light. To fix that problem and add a little interest to the design of the new bathroom, part of the wall between the shower and tub was replaced with a poly-carbonate panel that allows some light to shine through to the shower. But first, the existing wall had to be reframed to support the weight of the new panel.

1 Cut new support studs with a miter saw. Connect the new studs to the old ones with a right-angle driver using 2½-inch screws (photo A).

2 Determine the height of the new window. Then point a laser line (photo B) 1½ inches lower to account for the width of the framing board and mark that spot on the studs.

3 Cut through the existing studs at the mark with a reciprocating saw (photo C) and pull them out.

4 Drop in a framing board and make sure it's level and square. Screw the frame into place (photo D). The new panel was installed later, once the rest of the construction was done, to avoid damaging it (see pages 117-119).

A

B

C

D

You Will Need

- Circular saw
- Hole saw
- Drill
- Reciprocating saw
- Hammer
- Tape measure
- Pencil
- Concrete board
- Masonry screws
- Safety gloves and goggles

A

INSTALLING THE SHOWER PAN

Before tiling the shower you'll need to install a shower pan, which will have the right amount of slope for the water to drain properly.

1 Cut a piece of concrete board to fit the shower floor, then use a hole saw to remove a piece for the drainpipe to go through. Apply a bead of construction adhesive to the bottom of the cement board and drop it into place. Attach the board to the floor with masonry screws.

2 Cut away the excess drainpipe with a reciprocating saw fitted with a flexible 6-inch blade (photo A). The pipe should be flush with the concrete board.

3 Apply construction adhesive to the bottom of the shower base, making sure to cover each cleat and the area around the drain hole (photo B).

4 Press the shower pan into place on top of the concrete board. Apply pressure by walking and jumping on it until it feels steady.

5 Install the drain assembly. Use soapy water to help ease the rubber ring into place (photo C). Insert the drain cover.

B

C

A

B

INSTALLING THE SHOWER WALLS AND NICHE

1 With a circular saw, cut the concrete board to size. Use a hole saw to make cuts in the boards for the plumbing.

2 Attach the boards to the wall with porcelain-lined masonry screws. If the screws won't go in, pound them with a hammer to knock them into place (photo A, left) and then continue drilling. Make sure the screw head is countersunk just below the surface of the board.

3 Determine the height of the shower niche and mark that spot on the wall studs (photo B, left). Transfer the measurements to a piece of concrete board.

4 With a circular saw, make a plunge cut into the board along the marked lines and carefully make the cut-out for the niche (photo C).

5 Screw the board into place. Apply construction adhesive to the back and sides of the niche and insert it into the cement on the wall.

You Will Need

Tiles	6" taping knife	Rubber gloves
Batten board	¼" square-notch trowel	Safety goggles
Drill and screws	⅛" spacers	Concrete backerboard
Self-adhesive mesh tape	Wet saw	
Thinset mortar	Tile breaker	

▨ TILING THE SHOWER ▨

1 Screw a batten board into the wall to support the tiles. Later, when the tiles above it are set, the board will be removed and tiles put in its place.

2 Seal the seams in the concrete board with self-adhesive mesh tape (photo A). Mix a batch of thinset mortar and spread the mud over the tape with a 6 inch taping knife to fill the seams.

3 Using a ¼-inch square-notch trowel, spread the thinset on the rest of the wall (photo B). Cover only as much area as you can tile in 15 minutes. Use a premium thinset in a wet area like a shower, especially for large tiles.

4 Press the tiles against the wall, giving each a slight twist to create a suction that will hold them to the wall. Place ⅛-inch spacers between the tiles for consistent grout lines (photo C).

5 To make narrow cuts along the edges of the tile, use a wet saw. If you need to cut a tile in half, it can be faster to use a tile breaker. Simply score a line down the middle of the tile and apply pressure to split the tile. This doesn't work as well when you want to cut a small amount off a tile.

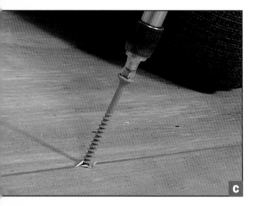

You Will Need

½" CDX plywood	Pencil	Deck screws
T-square	Chalk line	Concrete board
Circular saw	Drill	Masonry screws

INSTALLING A NEW SUBFLOOR

The existing subfloor was not strong enough to support the porcelain floor tiles, so Amy put down a new ½-inch plywood subfloor. If you tile over a bouncy or sagging subfloor, your tiles and grout will most likely crack over time. On top of the new subfloor, Amy added a layer of concrete board to further support the tiles.

1 Mark your cut lines on the plywood using a T-square (photo A). Cut the plywood to size, running the circular saw across the width of the board.

2 Using the original subfloor nails as a guide, mark the floor joist locations on the wall (photo B) so you'll know where to screw down the new subfloor once the old nails are covered.

3 Lay the first piece of plywood on the floor and fasten it with deck screws in a few spots to hold it in place. Then lay down the rest of the plywood pieces.

4 Using the marks you made on the walls, snap a chalk line on the plywood so you know where the floor joists are. Then drive deck screws every 8 inches along the line (photo C).

5 Bring in the concrete board and lay it over the plywood. Screw the board on the plywood using masonry screws that resist corrosion. Use one screw every 6 inches across the boards (photo D).

TIPS
DIY Network
Home Improvement

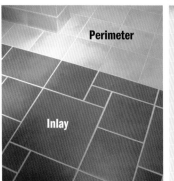

Perimeter

Inlay

Tile in the Right Order
Set the inlay tiles before the perimeter tiles. That way, if the walls aren't perfectly straight, you can cut the perimeter tiles to compensate for any imperfections. The cut edges will later be covered by base molding.

You Will Need

18", 12", and 8" tiles	¼" square-notch trowel
Tape measure	Thinset mortar
Ruler	⅛" spacers
Pencil	

LAYING FLOOR TILE WITH AN INLAID PATTERN

1 Decide where you want the inlay tile pattern and draw straight lines to mark the edges of the area (photo A).

2 Apply thinset to the concrete board with a ¼-inch square-notch trowel inside the lines of the inlay pattern. Be careful not to cover the layout lines.

3 Begin tiling the inlay area, setting each tile with a slight twisting motion to set it securely (photo B). Once the inlay is done, lay the surrounding field tiles.

You Will Need

Cardboard	Tape measure	Mask	Water-based polyurethane
Pencil	Clamps	Eye protection	
Utility knife	Scrap 2 x 4	Gloves	
Marker	Router	Sanding blocks	

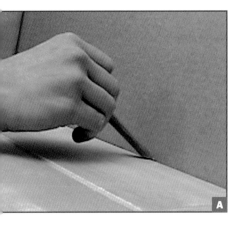

CUTTING THE SHOWER PANEL

A translucent, polycarbonate panel with spalike reed inserts was chosen to separate the shower from the tub. This panel will allow some much needed light into the shower area. Cutting and installing a special window like this is a fairly simple procedure.

1 Use cardboard from the shipping box to make a template of the window. Hold the cardboard up to the window opening and trace the outline onto the cardboard with a pencil (photo A). The lines don't need to be exact because you're cutting for size, not for shape, and you'll be cutting the panel a bit smaller than the opening.

2 Cut out the cardboard template with a utility knife. Place the template on the polycarbonate panel with the outside edges lined up and trace with a marker.

3 Measure and mark 1¾ inches outside the trace line, which is the distance between the router bit and the guide of the tool (photo B).

4 Line up a 2 by 4 along that second line and clamp it firmly to the panel. It will act as a fence for the tool.

5 You're going to make two passes with the router to get the cleanest cut possible. Set the depth of the router to half the depth of the panel. Start cutting, pushing firmly and moving fast enough so the heat from the router bit doesn't melt the polycarbonate (photo C). Then go back for the second pass with the router.

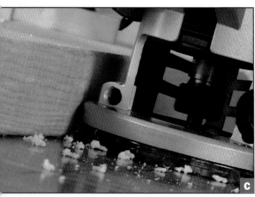

6 Use a sanding block to remove the sharp edges left by the router (photo D). Then, because this will be installed in a wet area, apply a coat of water-based polyurethane to the edges to ensure that no moisture will be absorbed by the panel. This way the natural reeds will stay dry.

You Will Need

- Closed-foam double-sided tape
- Aluminum U-channel
- Silicone
- Screen spline
- Spline roller

INSTALLING THE SHOWER PANEL

1 Cut pieces of aluminum U-channel to fit all four sides of the window opening. Apply a strip of closed-foam, double-sided tape to the bottom of each piece (photo A). Before you set them in place, make sure the tile is completely clean and dry. Otherwise the tape won't stick. Remove the cover strip on the bottom channel and press it into place on the tile surface.

2 Run a bead of silicone along the inside of the remaining three channels and press them onto the edges of the window. Bring the window over to the opening and slide it into place. Use the edge of a flat tool to press the channels against the tile (photo B), making sure each area has good contact.

3 Insert a strip of screen spline in the channel on the dry side of the window (photo C). This eliminates any movement of the panel and keeps it pressed firmly to the shower side of the channel, forming a watertight seal.

You Will Need

- Tape measure
- Pencil
- Level
- Screwdriver

HANGING CABINETS

These sleek, modern cabinets are meant to hang on the wall, and they come with their own mounting brackets. The homeowners decided to place them about 12 inches above the floor so there would be room for storage baskets above and below.

1 Measure the cabinet from top to bottom, then add the amount of space you want underneath when they're on the wall. Measure that total length on the wall, then mark the top, bottom, and center points with a pencil.

2 Take the center of the mounting bar that comes with the cabinet, line it up with the center mark on the wall, and mark the locations of the screw holes.

3 Punch holes on these marks with a screwdriver. Drive the anchors into the holes and attach the mounting bar to the wall with screws and washers (photo A).

4 Hang the cabinet brackets on the wall bar. Check for level (photo B) and tighten the screws from the inside of the cabinet.

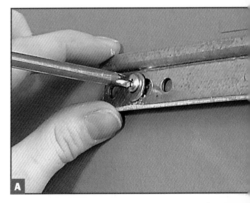

You Will Need

- Rock saw
- PVC pipe
- Flexible air hose
- Petroleum jelly
- Spanner wrench
- Teflon tape
- Wrench
- Screwdriver
- Plumber's putty
- Star wrench

INSTALLING THE JET TUB AIR PUMP

You'll need to find a location in an adjoining room to install the tub's air pump. You may choose a closet in a bedroom next door, the attic, or the garage. In this case, the master bathroom was right above the garage and the garage already had a utility room where the pump could be housed. Just be sure the air pump has access to plenty of fresh air. If it doesn't, you'll need to vent a second hose to an outside air source.

1 Standing in the garage, cut through the drywall below the bathroom with a rock saw. Make a hole big enough to feed the flexible air hose through. Cut a second access hole right next to the utility closet.

2 Fish one end of the hose up to the hole already made in the bathroom floor from the panel below that you just cut. Then feed the other end of the hose toward the utility room (photo A). Have a helper pull the other side through to the air pump (photo B).

3 Before hooking up the hose to the air pump, install an air check valve. This valve ensures that the air flows to the tub instead of back into the pump. Set the valve and use a stub of PVC pipe to couple the valve to the pump, twisting it into place.

4 Back upstairs in the bathroom, a plumber came in to install the tub filler. But the homeowners needed to attach it to the tub. First rub petroleum jelly on the O-ring to ensure a tight seal.

5 Place the supply lines on the pre-plumbed fixtures on the floor and tighten with a spanner wrench (photo C). Rub more petroleum jelly on the O-rings of the transition elbow (photo D) and tighten it onto the supply lines. Attach the faucet to the elbow, tightening with a wrench.

6 To install the drain basket, wrap Teflon tape around the threads (photo E, next page). Apply plumber's putty to the underside of the drain and push it into place in the tub. Use a star wrench to tighten down the drain basket.

7 Install the overflow assembly by fitting the overflow pipe and the screen onto the tub. Finally, insert the PVC air hose into the tub, connecting the air pump and the tub.

You Will Need

Drill	Anchors	Hammer
Silicone	Wood shim	Stainless-steel screws
Painter's tape		

INSTALLING THE SHOWER DOOR

1 First drill holes into the tile walls for the side rails. Run a bead of silicone on the underside of the threshold piece (photo A) and press it into place. You don't want to use any screws here because water can seep through and cause problems. Hold the threshold down with painter's tape so it doesn't move during the rest of the installation.

2 Tap plastic anchors into the pre-drilled holes in the wall and slide each side rail into the threshold piece. Screw the pieces into the walls with stainless-steel screws (photo B).

3 Drop rubber spacers into the channel on the left side of the threshold to hold the stationary panel of the door. Then slide the stationary panel into place and insert the center rail and top rail to hold it there.

4 Snap fillers into the threshold and the top rail where the swing door will go. These will keep water from collecting in the channel and give the frame a more finished look.

5 Use a wood shim (anything metal might scratch the glass) to push a glazing strip into the channel on both sides of the stationary glass panel (photo C). If one side is harder to squeeze in, spray some window cleaner on the glass to lubricate it.

6 Bring in the swing door. Slide the hinge into the side rail and threshold, then snap it into place.

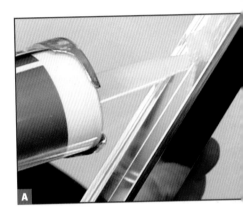

A

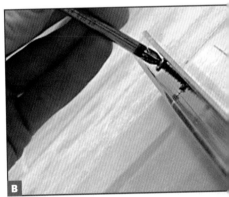

B

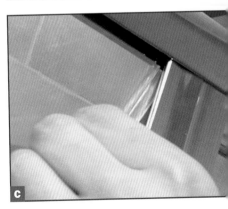

C

Color
CORRECTION

What if you have a sound bathroom with no structural problems but you just hate the way it looks? That was the case for these homeowners, whose 1950s bathroom was covered in blue and pink tile and tacky wallpaper that wasn't helping at all. Luckily, Amy found ways to change the look completely without breaking the bank on a major remodel.

◀ PROJECT SUMMARY ▶

The existing wall tile, countertop, sink, and bathtub were all professionally resurfaced. The floor tile was in good shape and now sparkles after being professionally cleaned and sealed. The vintage blue toilet couldn't be resurfaced, but since it was in good condition, the homeowners carefully removed it in the hopes of selling it online to someone who may be doing a period remodel. After the black fan-and-flower wallpaper was removed, the walls were painted a neutral color. Paired with the new almond tiles, counter, toilet, and tub, the room looked better already. A new faucet, tub fixtures, and accessories completed the transformation.

BEFORE: This pink and blue tiled bathroom with black wallpaper didn't work with the rest of the house.

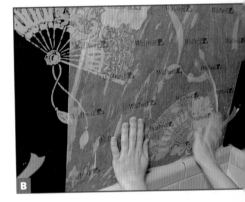

You Will Need

- Scoring tool
- Bucket
- Wallpaper removing solution
- Wallpaper removing sheets
- Putty knife
- Pressure sprayer

REMOVING WALLPAPER

Before you start removing wallpaper, try picking at the edge to see how easily it comes off. Some newer vinyl wallpapers will peel right off. If yours doesn't, you have several options, including using a steamer to loosen the glue or spraying on a chemical solution. In this bathroom, Amy and the homeowner used a product that softens the wallpaper with special sheets and solution.

1 Go over the wall thoroughly with a scoring tool, applying light pressure so the nick marks go only through the paper, not into the drywall (photo A).

2 Dip the sheets into a bucket of solution that consists of 1 ounce of dissolver mixed with 1 gallon of warm water. This solution is safe to handle with bare hands.

3 When the sheets are soaked, spread them on the walls, smoothing out any air bubbles from the top down (photo B). Continue laying the sheets across the wall, leaving a small gap between each one (that way, if one falls off, it won't take the rest with it).

4 After the sheets are on, use a pressure sprayer to douse them with more solution (photo C). Make sure you really soak them so the dissolver will seep into the wallpaper. Then wait about 15 minutes.

5 Remove the sheets from the wall and then peel off the wallpaper (photo D). Use a putty knife to scrape off any stubborn pieces.

SURFACE REFINISHING

Since the tile, tub, and sink were in pretty good condition, they were prime candidates for resurfacing. There are do-it-yourself resurfacing kits on the market, but the chemicals used are weaker and the new color simply covers the old materials rather than bonding to it. Professional resurfacing companies use much more powerful materials. They also etch the surface before spraying on the new color, which allows the color to penetrate into the old surface. The result is a smooth finish with the look and feel of porcelain. If these homeowners had hired professionals to remove and replace the old tile, tub, and countertop, it would have cost around $8,000. But for a bathroom their size, they paid only $1,000 for professional resurfacing. The following steps detail what was done.

1 The tub was scrubbed clean, and then an etching solution that contains powerful acids was applied to rough up and de-glaze the surface. Since these are strong chemicals, the professional wore a respirator, chemical gloves, and goggles.

2 After the etching solution was applied, it was worked into the surface with a nylon scrubbing brush (photo A). Over the next 15 minutes the solution went to work, opening up the porcelain so the finish coat would adhere. Then the solution was rinsed away with water. The tub was also wet sanded to remove any chalky residue that could keep the finish from adhering.

3 The last step of the prep was to repair any of the imperfections and cracks in the grout lines with a special putty applied with a razor blade (photo B). The hardened putty was then sanded to a perfectly smooth surface.

4 After prepping all the surfaces and masking the areas that were not to be painted, it was time to start refinishing. Because the refinishing spray is hazardous, the installer put a high-volume blower in the window to draw out most of the overspray and fumes. He also put on a protective suit, mask, goggles, and gloves.

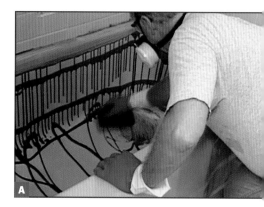

A

B

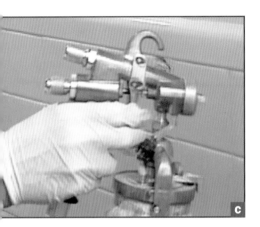

5 A white primer was sprayed on all the surfaces to be refinished. Once the primer was dry, the first coat of the new almond color was applied (photo C). This finish is made of a tough acrylic polyurethane that cures in about four hours. After four coats are applied, the job is done.

You Will Need

Tape measure	Screwdriver
Pencil	Anchors and screws
Hammer	Crescent rod
Laser level	

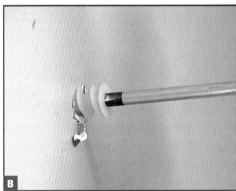

INSTALLING A CURVED SHOWER ROD

The homeowners chose to install a crescent rod that keeps the curtain farther away from you while you're showering.

1 To install the rod, measure 79 inches up from the floor (photo A), which is the standard height for a 72-inch shower curtain. Use a laser level to make sure the relative position of the end brackets is the same on both sides.

2 To mount the brackets, you can use easy anchors that you tap into the wall and then screw into place (photo B). These anchors tend to strip easily, so be careful not to over tighten the screws. Mount the brackets to the anchors.

3 Slide one end of the rod into the wall bracket and snug up the top and bottom screws. Insert the other end of the rod and tighten the bracket (photo C).

CONTEMPORARY

This large master bathroom was built as three separate rooms, which made it feel like a cramped maze. One end leads to the master bedroom and the other end to a guest room. To open up the space and make it as modern as the rest of the house, Amy and the homeowners tore down the interior walls, ripped out the existing cabinets and fixtures, and infused it with some much needed style.

BEFORE: Separate rooms made this large bathroom feel small, and the homeowners disliked the yellow and brown color scheme.

AFTER: The new bathroom functions much better as one continuous space.

AFTER: Swanky open vanities with glass countertops and integrated sinks give the new bathroom a modern look.

BEFORE: The dated countertop and sink had to go.

◀ PROJECT SUMMARY ▶

The old toilet and vanities were removed, and then to create a more spacious feeling, the interior walls that made the bathroom three small units were torn down. The original yellow bathtub was left in place but completely covered with a custom-fit acrylic surround. These homeowners really wanted a separate shower and chose to install a pre-plumbed, luxury corner shower with multiple body jets. Plumbing needed to be extended into the corner to make this happen.

On the walls of the shower and behind the vanity, they installed 12-by-12-inch honed travertine tile. For the floor, they chose an innovative snap-together porcelain tile that eliminates most of the hassle of tile setting. A pair of mahogany-stained console vanities topped with glass countertops and integrated sinks, sleek sconces, and a European push-button toilet complete the transformation.

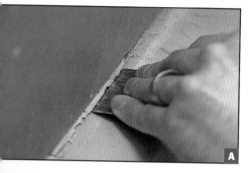

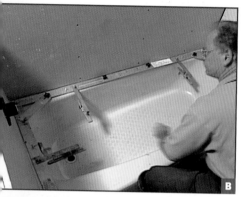

◣ INSTALLING THE ACRYLIC BATHTUB ◢

Because they have only one tub/shower in the house, the homeowners didn't want to completely demolish it and have to wait a long time for a new one to be installed. So they chose a quick and money-saving solution: a custom acrylic liner made to fit over any existing cast-iron or pressed-steel bathtub. The liners come in several colors and styles and are made of a material that won't crack or peel. Plus, the liner is installed in one day, reducing the number of times the homeowners had to shower at their gym. The matching acrylic surround can be placed directly over old wall tiles. But because there was an existing leak, the tiles from one wall were removed so the damage could be inspected and new green board (moisture-resistant drywall) put up. Luckily, the acrylic surround can go over two different surfaces as long as they are flat. Be sure to order a custom acrylic liner well in advance of your remodel, as the entire process takes four to six weeks. The acrylic bathtub liner will usually be installed by the company you order it from, but the following instructions will give you a solid understanding of how it's done.

1 Prepare the old tub by removing existing caulk (photo A), the drain, and fixtures, and then vacuum the tub clean.

2 The installer sets a metal template on the old tub to get its overall size and the contours of the existing walls (photo B). The template is then taken outside and set on the new tub liner, which is made with excess shelf area that is meant to be trimmed before installation. A jigsaw is used to cut the liner to fit. Then a pilot hole is cut with a spade bit for the drain and overflow in the new tub.

3 The cut liner is placed over the old tub to check for fit (photo C), and then the drain and overflow holes are routed using the old tub holes as a guide.

4 Once the holes are cut, a black primer is painted around the rim of the old tub and the bottom of the new liner. This serves as the surface for the adhesive tape.

TIPS | DIY Network Home Improvement

Cleaning
To clean acrylic surfaces, do not use any abrasive or any caustic cleaners (cleaners that are capable of burning, corroding, dissolving or eating away by chemical action). Use an all-purpose cleaner instead.

5 Strips of butyl tape are placed on the outline of the old tub (photo D, previous page) to act as a sealant and adhesive. The tape is also placed over the entire underside of the new liner, and then the tape backings are removed before the liner is set in place.

6 A generous amount of flowable silicone is applied to the edges of the old tub (photo E).

7 The liner is placed over the old tub, and then the entire surface is walked on in order to adhere the liner to the old tub and to remove any air bubbles (photo F). The drain and overflow need to be put in quickly before the adhesive dries.

INSTALLING THE ACRYLIC TUB SURROUND

The homeowner removed the tiles from the wall that had a leak problem and replaced the existing underlayment with new water-resistant green board. The other wall still had the old tile. The acrylic surround can go over both surfaces because they are solid walls, but the tile didn't reach all the way to the ceiling, so a piece of plywood was attached above the tiles to create a continuous, solid surface.

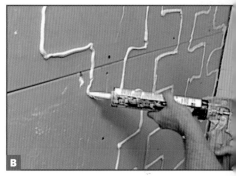

1 To install the surround, measure the height and width of the wall and cut the panel to fit using a jigsaw with a medium-tooth blade (photo A).

2 Apply a thermal expansion adhesive to the entire wall in a zigzag pattern, 2 to 3 inches apart (photo B). The adhesive allows for expansion and contraction, and it will prevent the panels from separating from the wall.

3 Center the acrylic panel on the wall and smooth it out by hand (photo C). Once the panel is in place, seal the edges with silicone.

You Will Need

- Concrete backerboard
- 1¼" self-setting screws
- 360-degree laser level
- Tile
- Tape measure
- Batten board
- Thinset mortar
- Drill and paddle mixer
- ³⁄₁₆" V-notch trowel
- ⅛" spacers
- Wet saw with diamond blade

TIPS | DIY Network Home Improvement

Holes for Plumbing
Cut any holes in the concrete backerboard needed for plumbing before hanging the board on the wall.

◢ TILING THE WALLS ◣

The homeowners chose 12-by-12-inch travertine stone tiles for their bathroom walls. The tiles are honed, meaning that one side has been polished to a smooth finish. It's important to seal natural stone tiles before installation, as mortar and grout can easily stain them. You'll also want to reseal the tiles periodically to make sure moisture doesn't seep in.

In this bathroom remodel, the new shower was placed where there used to be a door leading to the guest room. Since this area was never used as a shower before, the drywall was removed so that new plumbing could be brought in. After the plumbing was completed, the homeowners took the opportunity to add insulation to the exterior and interior walls, both for weather protection and noise reduction. On top of the insulation they attached panels of desiccant packages, which will absorb any built-in moisture in the walls. Then polyethylene sheeting was stapled to the studs to cover the insulation and protect the interior walls, should any moisture ever seep in from under the tiles. If you are installing tiles in your shower surround and don't have an open wall to start with, it's still best to start the process with new backerboard underlayment.

A

B

1 Attach concrete backerboard to the wall studs using 1¼-inch self-setting screws (photo A). Now you have a flat, even, water-resistant surface for your wall tiles.

2 Measure the walls and use a laser level to mark a starting line. Do a dry run of the tile arrangement on the floor to make sure you won't end up with a small sliver in an obvious place. It's a good idea to temporarily screw a wood batten board onto the bottom of the wall to use as a guide for your first row of tiles (photo B). It will give you an even, level surface to start with, and it will support the heavy tiles before the mortar dries.

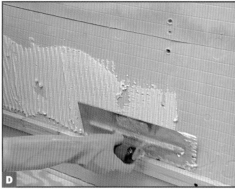

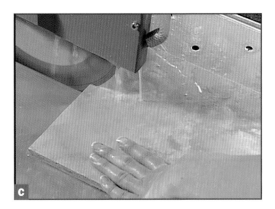

3 Make cuts as you go using a wet saw with a diamond blade (photo C). It should cut through a soft natural stone like travertine with no problems.

4 Mix thinset mortar with an electric drill fitted with a paddle mixer until it's the consistency of peanut butter. Then use a 3/16-inch V-notch trowel to spread the mortar on the wall (photo D). Hold the trowel at a consistent angle for even ridges.

5 Starting at the batten board, set each tile with a slight twisting motion and use 1/8-inch spacers between the tiles to get an even grout line (photo E).

6 Wash the tiles with a sponge when finished to remove any dust or excess thinset. Once the mortar is dry, grout the walls (photo F).

You Will Need

Tile	Knee pads
Foam underlayment	Grout
Cellophane tape	Rubber float
Table saw	Sponge
Safety goggles	Bucket of warm water
Mask	

TILING THE FLOOR

When tiling a floor, you usually have to install a concrete board underlayment and then spread thinset mortar to adhere the tiles to the board. In this bathroom remodel, the homeowners chose a unique product that makes tile setting much easier. These ceramic tiles are attached to a high-density fiberboard backer, so no additional plywood or concrete backerboard underlayment is needed. Two tiles are on each piece of board, which makes installation twice as fast. The edges of the boards have tongue-and-groove panels, allowing you to simply snap the pieces together.

1 Before laying the tile, make sure the subfloor is smooth and even. Then roll out a foam underlayment, silver side down (photo A). The foam underlayment acts as a moisture and cold barrier, keeping the subfloor dry and the tile warm. Use cellophane tape to attach the underlayment to the subfloor, and to hold the pieces together.

2 Measure, mark, and cut the tiles to fit the room. A table saw will cut through the ceramic tile and fiberboard backer. Stagger the tiles as you go so the edges will lock together more effectively (photo B).

3 This flooring system comes with its own grout in a pressurized can. Squeeze the grout into the tile joints (photo C).

4 Hold a rubber float at a 45-degree angle and smooth it over the grout (photo D). Spread any excess into open spaces in the joints. Then wipe the excess grout off the tiles with a sponge before it dries.

You Will Need

- Shower components
- Safety goggles
- Hammer drill with ¼" masonry bit
- Hammer
- Plastic glass anchors
- Wrench

- Heavy-duty suction cup
- Nylon shims
- Hex-head bolts
- Hex-head wrench
- Level
- Marker

- Drill
- Screwdriver and screws
- 1½" screws
- PVC saw
- 2 X 4 blocks
- 1 X 2 cleats

INSTALLING THE GLASS SHOWER SURROUND

The homeowners chose a luxury corner shower with multiple body jets for their new bathroom. Since there was no shower in this spot before, lots of plumbing work needed to happen before the shower unit could be installed. They ran a new drain line and rerouted supply lines in the floor to make room for a new P-trap. Then copper supply lines were run up the walls and soldered to the valves and multiple shower heads. Since this shower system has many jets, all that plumbing took a while to do. Fortunately, the new shower system comes pre-plumbed, so once it's in place, the supply lines just need to be soldered together and the shower will be ready to go.

Installing a shower system like this does take a lot of plumbing work, so if you're unsure about that process it's a good idea to hire a plumber. But the shower system itself is fairly easy to assemble. The first step is to install the shower base.

A

B

1 Line up the drainpipe coming out of the floor with the drain hole on the shower base and carefully set the base down in place to dry fit (photo A).

2 Remove the shower base and cut the drainpipe with a PVC saw so that it's flush with the subfloor.

3 Cut and insert 2-by-4 blocks between the wall studs near the floor. These blocks go in before the shower base and will later support concrete backerboard. Then screw 1-by-2 cleats into the studs, about 4 inches off the floor (photo B). These cleats will support the shower base flange.

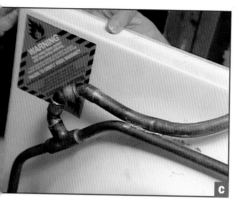

5 Screw the drain assembly to the shower base. Before putting the shower base in place, sweat the supply pigtail to the shower base pipe (photo C) and then slide the shower base into place.

6 Use hand soap and water to lubricate the gasket and slide it into the drain (photo D). Screw in the caulking nut using the spanning wrench that came with the shower system. Next screw on the strainer.

7 Screw retaining brackets to the backerboards in the wall using 1½-inch screws (photo E). This will hold the base in place.

8 Once the shower base is in place, the plumbing is hooked up, and the walls are tiled, you're ready to install the doors and doorposts. The glass panels are attached to the tile walls with support brackets. Using a hammer drill with a ¼-inch masonry bit, drill holes for the glass support brackets in the wall (photo F), then tap in the plastic anchors.

9 While a helper holds the doorpost, attach the flex hose in the shower post to the fitting in the shower base using a wrench, being careful not to overtighten (photo G). This hose will bring the water from the base into the doorposts and then up to the four body jets. Temporarily stand the post in place, using the cam locking system at the base.

10 Now the first glass panel can be installed. To handle them safely, use a heavy-duty suction cup to lift each panel into place (photo H). Heavy-duty suction cups hold up to 600 pounds and are available at most rental centers for about $15 per day.

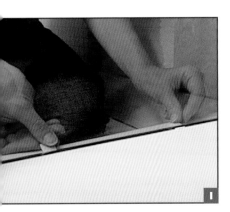

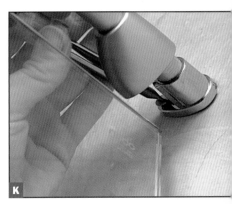

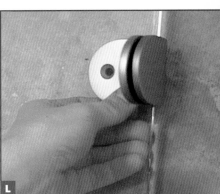

11 Carefully slide the glass panel into the channel in the doorpost, which is lined with a silicone glazing strip. Once the glass is in position, gently turn the doorpost until you hear the cam at the base lock into place.

12 Insert small nylon shims under the glass to hold it temporarily in place (photo I). Then repeat the entire process for the glass panel on the other side.

13 Use the curved tie-rod piece to tie the two doorposts together (photo J). The rod attaches to the top of the doorposts with small hex-head bolts. Then attach another short tie-rod from the doorposts to the walls in the same way, but don't anchor them to the walls quite yet.

14 Use a level to check for plumb on each post, then make a mark on the wall where the bracket will attach.

15 Drill holes on each mark and screw the brackets into the holes (photo K). Slide the bracket cover into place.

16 Attach the brackets that will hold the glass panels to the wall (photo L).

17 To install the door, remove the hinge cover plate and center the hole in the door on the bushing in the hinge. Then replace the cover plate and tighten the assembly with a hex bolt. There's room to adjust the tilt of the door if it doesn't close properly.

HIGH-TECH

It's out with the old and in with the new in this high-tech makeover. The master bathroom in this 1970s home may have been groovy back then, but today it was a maze of green foil wallpaper and shag carpeting. Both the toilet and the sunken bathtub surrounded by rough stone were situated in front of floor-to-ceiling windows, which didn't provide much privacy. Only a major remodel could save this room.

BEFORE: An odd mix of styles, from the sunflower chandelier to the foil wallpaper, made this bathroom an eyesore.

AFTER: A double vanity with vessel sinks and granite countertops hover above a stamped concrete floor. What a difference!

PROJECT SUMMARY

The homeowner was already remodeling his entire house, so he used the contractor and crew he had on site to demolish the existing bathroom, remove the mazelike interior walls, replace the large windows with smaller ones set high on the walls, and do the rough plumbing and electrical work. The homeowner decided to go all out and create the ultimate bachelor bathroom, complete with high-tech heated concrete floors, a raised air-jet tub, a steam shower with microfiber lighting, an electronic toilet, and an LCD television that suddenly appears through a mirror when you turn it on.

This was an expensive project. Materials alone cost over $45,000. But the homeowner saved about $15,000 by doing some of the work himself. People often think they need to hire professionals for either all of a project or none of it, but that's not the case. Chose the parts of the project you feel comfortable with, enjoy, and have time to do, and then hire out the rest.

AFTER: The raised jetted tub is easier to get in and out of (below) and the steam shower is the ultimate in luxury (right).

BEFORE: A sunken tub in front of a window offered no privacy, and the stone surround was rough on hands and feet.

You Will Need

Tub outline template	8-penny ring shanks
Lumber	Level
Chalk line	Adhesive
Tape measure	Staple gun
Safety goggles	Marker
Gloves	Drill with paddle bit
Miter saw	Jigsaw
Nail gun	Hammer

◢ BUILDING THE TUB DECK ◣

The original bathtub sat beneath the floor, so when it was removed, it left a large hole. Eventually that hole will be filled in to support the weight of the new tub, but for now it's left open for easier access to the plumbing. The hole is covered with a sheet of plywood so no one falls in during construction. The new tub will be raised on a 22-inch platform, so Amy and the homeowner got to work on framing the tub deck.

1 New jet tubs like this will come with a spec sheet that can be used to draw a diagram of where to place the tub. Start by taking some measurements to mark off where the cabinetry will meet the tub deck and then snap a chalk line to make the mark. Do the same for the outside of the deck.

2 Cut 2 by 4s to the length and height of the deck to make the framework. Then nail them together and nail the frames to the floor (photo A). Be sure to check the frame with a level as you go.

3 Mark the height of the frame on the wall and nail in a 2-by-4 cleat at that point (photo B). Add another support 2 by 4 across the frame if you are using more than one sheet of plywood to cover the deck. Make sure the plywood fits before moving on.

TIPS | DIY Network
Home Improvement

Chalk Lines
You can spray hair spray over the chalk line to keep it in place.

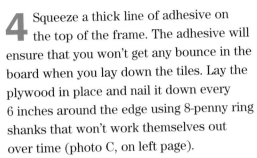

4 Squeeze a thick line of adhesive on the top of the frame. The adhesive will ensure that you won't get any bounce in the board when you lay down the tiles. Lay the plywood in place and nail it down every 6 inches around the edge using 8-penny ring shanks that won't work themselves out over time (photo C, on left page).

5 Lay out the tub template to determine its placement on the deck, staple it to the plywood, and then mark with a pen all the way around (photo D).

6 Drill starter holes with a paddle bit just inside the mark, then use a jigsaw to cut around the template (photo E).

7 Use a hammer to pound out the inner plywood, leaving the hole for the tub (photo F).

You Will Need

Broom and dustpan	15 lb. standard roofing felt	Ohm meter
Vacuum	Knee pads	Scissors
Safety goggles	Hammer stapler	Staple gun
Gloves	Hammer	

IN-FLOOR ELECTRIC HEAT SYSTEM

The homeowner decided on a colored and stamped concrete floor. Underneath will be an electric radiant heat system, which will make the cold concrete nice and toasty before he comes in for his morning shower. The radiant heat system comes in coil mesh strips that are installed on the subfloor. The homeowner sent his floor plan to the radiant heat company that makes the system, and it sent him the right number of coil mesh strips and an installation plan.

1 The subfloor must be completely clean before you install the radiant heat system. Sweep and vacuum the floor until no dust or dirt is left, and be sure there are no protruding elements in the floor. Lay down standard roofing felt (photo A) and staple it in place. Then go back and pound down all the staples with a hammer until they are below the surface.

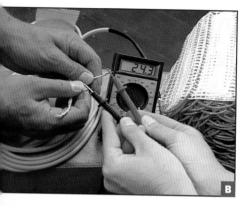

2 It's very important to test the radiant heat system at least four times during the installation process. You wouldn't want to pour concrete over it and then find out the system doesn't work. Test it for the first time right out of the box to make sure it wasn't damaged during shipping. A tag on each matted row of coils will have the numbers of the resistance test that was done at the factory. Test each mat with an ohm meter (photo B) and make sure your numbers are within 10 percent of the numbers the company sent you. The heat system comes with a chart where you can record your tests as you go.

3 Lay out the mats according to the plan (photo C), cutting the mesh at the end of the room for a return. Make sure you don't cut or nick the wires in the mesh when you cut. Then staple down the mesh, again avoiding the wires completely.

4 When all the mats are in place, secure the lead wires to the floor (photo D). Weave the temperature sensor through the mesh. An electrical inspector needs to check the floor warming system before you put down your flooring.

You Will Need

Concrete	Heavy-duty drill with mixing bit
Color additive	5-gal. bucket
Rubber stamps	¼" gauge rake
Safety goggles and mask	Large rubber squeegee

POURING A CONCRETE FLOOR

A concrete floor is a great choice for a modern, high-tech bathroom. But standard gray concrete is a little dull, so this concrete floor will be colored and stamped to look like natural stone. The finished floor will be ½ inch thick, but if you poured the full ½ inch at once, the concrete might crack. Therefore, it is poured in two ¼-inch layers. The first will cover the heat system, and then the top layer will be colored and stamped. It's a good idea to pour the first layer over the heat system and then wait to do the finish layer until the rest of the construction work on the bathroom is completed.

1 Insert 1-by lumber strips around the perimeter of the room to keep the wet concrete from getting in other areas. Mix the concrete according to the directions using a mixing bit on a heavy-duty drill. The result should be the consistency of a thick pancake batter.

2 Pour the concrete over the subfloor, then go over it with a ¼-inch gauge rake for a level finish (photo A).

3 Once all the concrete is spread out, go over the area with a large rubber squeegee to smooth any peaks and to close any lines left by the gauge rake (photo B). If any wires from the heating system are sticking up, you can pin them down with wire staples and then remove the staples when the concrete is dry. Don't worry if this causes a bumpy finish, as it will be covered by the top layer of concrete.

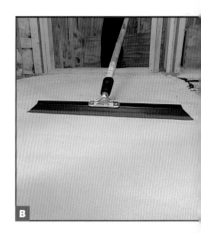

FINISH COAT OF CEMENT

There are different color and finish options for your concrete floor. The rubber stamps you use to texture the concrete are imprinted from natural materials. The distributor can send you samples. To get a feel for the process of stamping a concrete floor, pour a few strips outside and try out different stamps until you're confident enough to try it on the bathroom floor. To add color, you can either mix a pigment into the wet concrete or brush acid wash over the floor once it's been stamped. In this project, integral pigment was used.

The finish coat of concrete is made up of two compounds that get mixed together on the floor. The first mix is a thin bonding agent that will help provide good adhesion between the base coat and the finish coat. The second mix is the polymer concrete to which you will add the pigment. Like paint, you will mix it to a preset ratio until you get the color you want.

1 Run tape around the bottom edge of the room to protect the walls from the concrete. After making sure the first layer of concrete is nice and clean, pour the bonding agent in a small area and smooth it out with a rubber squeegee (photo A).

2 The colored concrete mix goes on top of that. Spread it with a gauge rake, which has small teeth that can be adjusted to the proper depth (photo B). Then smooth this layer out with the rubber squeegee.

3 Let the second coat cure for a couple of hours before you start stamping. Test it by pressing your thumb into it. If it has a little give but doesn't release onto your thumb, it's ready to go. Spray the bottom of the rubber stamps with the chemical release that comes with the system to prevent it from sticking to the concrete. Then lay the rubber stamps on the slightly soft concrete and walk on the top to impress the pattern (photo C). Start in the corner and work your way out of the room. Be sure to place the stamps perpendicular to each other, overlapping a little on the edges, to create a more random pattern. Continue this process all the way around the room.

You Will Need

Safety goggles	Screws
Hammer drill	Gloves
D'VersiBit	Level
Copper pipes	Marker
Plumber's tape	Anchors
Screw gun	Hammer

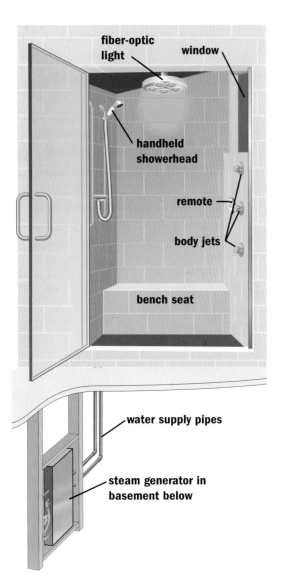

fiber-optic light

window

handheld showerhead

remote

body jets

bench seat

water supply pipes

steam generator in basement below

▰ INSTALLING THE STEAM SHOWER ▰

Most people think that plumbing a steam shower is beyond the scope of a do-it-yourself project, but it's really not much different from installing any other plumbing device. It has a steam generator with water in and water out lines, a drain, and a safety valve, just like on a water heater. The steam generator needs to go within 25 feet of the shower. You could put it in a bathroom wall, but then you'd have to create an access panel. In this project, the basement under the bathroom was the best choice because it provided a straight shot to the shower and was close to water and electrical sources for the house. Once the steam generator and thermostat control are mounted to the wall in the basement, call in a plumber and an electrician to make those final connections.

This is a particularly high-tech steam shower, with plenty of remote controls for its various functions. There is a main control for the mister steam that allows you to program the time and temperature in advance, and it will be installed right inside the shower door. There is also a remote control so that you can change the time or temperature without getting up. It has an on-off switch that you place on the inside door of the bathroom so that you can turn it on before you are ready to go in and take a shower. There's even a reservoir in the steam head where you can place aromatherapy oils to enjoy during your steam. The overall shower plan includes:

◢ A large window in the shower to let in light.

◢ A bench seat the entire width of the shower.

◢ The walls and bench will be tiled with a flamed granite-style porcelain, and slate tile will cover the floor.

◢ The steam head mounts 6 inches off the floor near the door.

◢ The wall-mounted remote for the steam shower is by the bench.

◢ A handheld showerhead is mounted on the left wall, and there are three body jets under the window.

◢ The water shower will be controlled by an electronic shower system keypad instead of faucets.

◢ And the real topper: a fiber-optic light.

1 Since the steam generator, thermostat, and computer box that control the system will be installed in the basement, holes are drilled in the subfloor for wires and copper supply pipes. There isn't much room to the left and right of the shower door opening, so a D'VersiBit is used to get into tight spaces (photo A). Feed the thermostat control wires from the basement up through the drilled hole.

2 The next step is to nail backerboards between the 2 by 4's in the shower every 6 inches up the wall to hold the supply lines in place (photo B). Mark the heights where the body jets will be placed and drop the supply lines into the previously drilled holes.

3 Make sure the copper pipes are plumb before attaching them to the backerboards with plastic anchor clips (photo C). Do the same thing on the other side of the shower to run a line for the handheld showerhead and any other supply lines.

4 A contractor installed the fiber-optic showerhead. Even though light is coming out through the showerhead, there is no electricity in it. A 75-watt halogen light bulb sits in a box that is hooked up to an electrical source in the basement. The bulb's light shines through a color wheel and then into the fiber-optic cables that run from the box through the floor, up the wall, and into the showerhead. As the light flows out of the showerhead, the water joins it, giving the illusion of different-colored water (photo D).

A

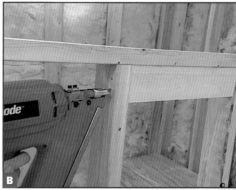
B

C

D

INSTALLING THE WATERPROOF SHOWER SYSTEM

A contractor put in the drain for the shower and ran the copper pipes that will supply the showerhead and body jets. Then the shower exhaust fan was installed. Normally, bathroom exhaust fans are located right above the vent that is visible on your ceiling, which is why you can hear the fan so clearly. This homeowner chose a system that locates the fan in a more remote area of the ceiling, cutting down on that noise. Once all the plumbing and electrical work are done, the shower walls can be framed and finished.

The walls behind a steam shower are particularly vulnerable to water damage, so special measures were taken to make sure the underlayment stays dry. Normally, shower walls consist of tile, mortar, or concrete backerboard. In this shower, a waterproof membrane was installed over the backerboard, giving it an extra layer of moisture protection.

1 To adhere the membrane to the concrete backerboard, mix a batch of standard, non-modified thinset mortar, which has no latex additive and will therefore cure more quickly. Mix it to a fairly thin pancake-batter consistency (photo A).

2 Soak the backerboard with a wet sponge before applying the thinset mortar so they won't absorb too much moisture from it (photo B).

3 Spread the thinset mortar on the wall using a ³⁄₁₆-inch V-notch trowel (photo C).

4 The membrane is made out of polyethylene and is easy to cut with a utility knife. Cut it to fit the walls and ceiling. Hang the membrane on the wall like wallpaper. Smooth it with your hand first, then with a clean flat finish trowel, working from the center out, to remove all the air bubbles (photo D).

5 Once the walls are covered, you are ready to put the polystyrene pan on the floor. This preformed pan can be cut to fit your shower floor, and it creates a nice slope down to the drain area. Apply a thicker batch of thinset mortar onto the floor and spread it on the pan using a 1/4-by-3/8-inch square-notch trowel this time. After laying the pan into the thinset mortar, wiggle it a bit to set it in the mud (photo E).

6 Apply more thinset to the drain hole and drop in the drain flange (photo F). It will be connected later to the drainpipe below.

7 Cover the floor tray and the ceiling with the membrane, using the same procedure as described above, and then do all the corners. The entire steam shower will then be watertight and you are ready to tile.

You Will Need

Tile materials	Grinder with diamond blade	3/16" cord
Safety goggles	Tape measure	1/4" x 1/4" square-notch trowel
Batten board	Pencil	
Screw gun and screws	Fully modified white thinset mortar	Sponge
Laser level		Wet saw
Large plastic bucket	Paddle mixer	
Grease pencil	Gloves	

◢ TILING THE TUB DECK ◣

The homeowner chose a porcelain tile from Italy that looks like granite, but it is approximately half the price of real stone. The larger tiles will be installed around the tub area, and smaller matching tiles will go around the wall. In any tiling project, the first tiles you set are the most important. To ensure the tiles end up straight, use a batten board as a starting line at the bottom of your surface.

1 Measure the height of the tiles and use a self-leveling laser to establish a line where the bottom edge of the tiles will go. Then screw a batten board into the studs in the tub deck to support the first layer of tiles. Do a dry layout of the tiles to decide on the best configuration. Make any cuts with a wet saw.

2 Mix a batch of fully modified white thinset mortar. Use a 1/4-by-1/4-inch square-notch trowel to apply a thick layer of mortar to the front (vertical) portion of the tub deck. The batten board will keep the tiles from moving down as the mortar dries.

3 Place the tiles using a piece of wet 3/16-inch cord as a spacer (photo A). Leave the cords in place for 20 minutes and then remove them. Wipe any excess mortar off the tiles with a sponge before it begins to dry.

THE EFFECT ON YOUR HOME'S SYSTEMS

With the new steam shower and large jet tub, the homeowner's 50-gallon tank is not going to be enough. You have several options for water heaters, including large commercial units or simply adding a second 50-gallon water heater next to your first one. This homeowner chose a tankless water heater that is piped inline. The water travels through the main water heater to the tankless system and then out into the bathroom. The tankless water heater acts as a backup and does not actually use any electricity unless you are running out of hot water. But when it is on, it takes 120 amps and 240 volts, which is a lot of electricity.

If you need an additional hot-water tank for a large project, chances are you'll also need additional electricity for things like a steam shower, electric radiant heating, or a jet tub. Ask an electrician to check whether you have the available amps on your electrical panel. If you do not, the electric company may need to come out and pull more power from the main lines, which can cost several thousand dollars. Be sure to think about these issues before deciding on the elements of your bathroom remodel so that the extra cost doesn't catch you by surprise.

INSTALLING AN ELECTRIC TOILET

This electronic toilet has an automatic seat lifter, a heated seat, a washer, and a dryer. It even flushes and cleans itself. But it doesn't install itself!

1 Insert the closet bolts and then the wax ring (photo A).

2 This toilet comes with its own flange assembly that bolts to the floor (photo B). Once that is in place, you are ready for the toilet base and the seat. Consider bringing in a professional to hook up the water and electrical lines.

You Will Need

Safety goggles	Hammer drill
Laser level	Jigsaw
Pencil	Tape
Tape measure	Wrench
Hole saw	Sink hardware
Lumber and shims	

▰ INSTALLING THE CABINETS AND SINKS ▰

The cherry cabinets will hang from the wall 16 inches off of the floor, and four slabs of granite will act as a countertop—one on each of the vanities, one on the medicine cabinet, and one on the new knee wall that separates the sinks from the toilet.

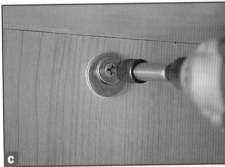

1 Using a laser level, mark the level line for the countertops. Then find a plumb line through the center of the wall-mounted spout to make sure the sinks and faucets will be centered (photo A).

2 Mark the drain location on the back of the cabinet and then use a hole saw to make an opening for the drain pipe (photo B).

> **TIPS** | DIY Network Home Improvement
>
> **Laser Line**
> Mark the laser line with a pencil so you can always see the reference line even if the laser light is blocked during installation.

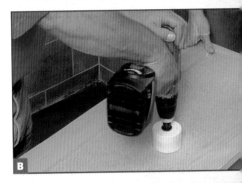

3 Because these cabinets will be attached 16 inches off the floor and have no legs, stack some lumber to hold them in position until they are attached. Use shims to adjust the height. Once they are in position, screw the cabinets to the wall with a hammer drill (photo C). When drilling your pilot holes, mark off the drill bit with tape (or use a stop collar) so you can watch to see that you don't go too far into the wall. Secure with washers and screws. (A piece of backerboard installed before the wall was tiled holds the cabinets firmly in place.)

4 The stone countertops already have cutouts for the sinks, but the cabinets do not. Place the countertops on the cabinets and mark the sink drain holes. Cut out the holes with a jigsaw (photo D).

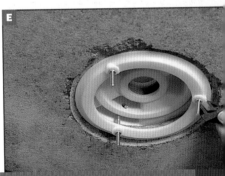

5 Attach the surface-mount sinks to the countertops with the J-bolts and retaining rings that came with the sinks (photo E, from under the sink). Then attach the faucets according to the manufacturer's instructions.

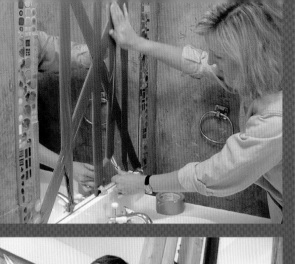

3

Basic Techniques

Are you inspired yet? You probably have your gloves on and are ready for action! Before you start tearing down the old wallpaper and swinging that sledgehammer, there are a few basic techniques you should read about.

In this final chapter, you'll learn how to demolish your bathroom safely and responsibly. No doubt you'll find yourself with a few walls to repair so there's information on how to patch them, as well as on repairing tiles and adding finishing touches like crown molding. And finally, a detailed plumbing section will take you step-by-step through the installations that will get your bathroom up and running.

By the end of this chapter, you will have the skills needed to dive into your own bathroom remodel.

Let the transformation begin!

You Will Need

- Rubber gloves
- Large sponge
- Wet/dry shop vac
- Bucket
- Wrench
- Hammer pliers
- Pliers
- Rags
- Scraper

DEMOLITION

Before doing any demolition work, be sure you protect yourself. Wear pants and long-sleeved shirts, heavy gloves, and goggles to avoid injury from flying debris. If you're using a loud power tool, wear earplugs. And if you're removing walls or floors, wear a respirator so you don't inhale too much dust. Use extreme caution when cutting into walls and floors so you don't hit any pipes or wires.

REMOVING A TOILET

1 Turn off the water. If there is no shutoff valve behind your toilet, the main water supply valve will need to be turned off.

2 Once the water supply is off, flush the toilet a couple of times to empty the tank. Use a sponge to soak up any remaining water in the tank and the bowl. Use a wet/dry shop vac for this if you have one (photo A). Wring out the sponge into a bucket and throw that water down the shower drain.

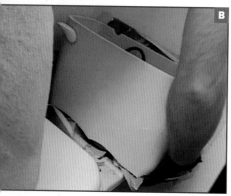

3 Place the bucket behind the toilet under the water supply line and use a wrench to disconnect the line from the tank. The bucket will catch any water still in the pipe.

4 If you're saving the toilet, first unscrew the two nuts under the tank. Bend at the knees and lift the tank off the bowl. Set it down on a towel. If you're throwing the toilet away, hit inside the tank near the bolts with a hammer until it breaks free from the bowl (photo B).

5 To remove the bowl, unscrew the two closet flange nuts and bolts that secure the bowl to the floor. Firmly rock the toilet back and forth to release the bowl from the wax ring. Or whack it with a hammer to break it into little pieces.

6 Lift the bowl off the flange. Quickly stuff a rag into the drain hole to stop any sewer gases from coming into the room.

7 Remove the old wax ring with pliers (photo C) and scrape off any remnants before installing a new one.

You Will Need

Bucket	Scraper
Rag	Crowbar
Wrench	Screwdriver

▰ REMOVING A SINK ▰

1 To remove a sink, first you must disconnect the faucet. Put a bucket under the P-trap. Use a wrench to loosen the compression fittings that connect the P-trap to the tailpipe and drainpipe, and unscrew them with your fingers (photo A). Once the drainpipe is removed, stuff a rag into the pipe leading to the wall to block any sewer gases.

2 Turn off the water supply, either to the sink (photo B) or to the house if you have no dedicated shutoff valves. Then detach the hot and cold water supply lines (photo C).

3 Unscrew the nuts holding the faucet to the sink from below. Or go straight to removing the sink and the faucet will come with it (photo D). If you have an undermount sink, unscrew the clips holding the sink to the underside of the counter. If you have a self-rimming sink, use a scraper to break the caulk seal and then pry it up with a crowbar.

TIPS | DIY Network Home Improvement

Reuse and Recycle Centers

Before you start demolishing your bathroom, check to see whether your local community has a building materials reuse or recycling center. Some centers take things like intact toilets, vanities, and doors, and will give you a tax write-off to donate them. The centers then sell your items to other homeowners and builders who are renovating older homes. Materials like tile, drywall, plaster, plumbing, and wiring can be taken to building recycling centers and made into something that someone else can use. So don't just add to the landfills—recycle anything you can.

A

B

REMOVING A BATHTUB

1 Turn off the water supply. Unscrew the fixtures and remove the overflow plate.

2 The easiest way to get an old cast-iron tub out of the bathroom is to break it into pieces with a sledgehammer (photo A). Wear eye protection and heavy gloves.

3 Remove manageable pieces one at a time (photo B). When you get to the edge, run a utility knife along the caulk to separate the tub from the wall.

TIPS | DIY Network Home Improvement

Rent a Trash Bin

If you can't find a reuse center in your area to take your old fixtures to, you will probably have a large amount of construction debris to get rid of. Depending on the scope of your remodel, you may need to rent a trash bin to dispose of any materials that cannot be recycled. Check with your local garbage service to see what construction materials cannot be disposed of in this way.

REMOVING TILE WALL

Place the tip of a pry bar at the top of a tile and hit the pry bar with a hammer (photo A, below). This should remove the tile without doing excessive damage to the wall. Then scrape away any remaining thinset.

A

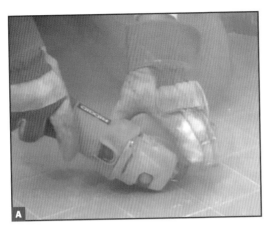

REMOVING FLOOR TILE

If you want to save and reuse the tiles, cut around the grout lines with a rotary tool (see page 157) and use a pry bar to remove each piece. If you don't want to save them and you want to remove the tiles but not the subfloor, it's much quicker to smash them. Place a towel over the tiles so the shards don't fly across the room, and then hit the tiles with a hammer. Be sure to wear eye protection and heavy gloves. A hand scraper will remove any remaining adhesive from the floor.

If you need to remove the tiles and subfloor, cut out 2-foot sections (photo A), use a pry bar to lift each piece up (photo B), and remove the floor one section at a time (photo C).

REMOVING A MIRROR

Before taking a mirror off the wall, apply a good amount of duct tape (photo A, left) so that if it breaks during the move it won't shatter into shards. Use heavy work gloves and carefully lift it off the wall with a helper.

You Will Need

- Drop cloths/plastic sheeting
- Masking tape
- Respirator
- Safety goggles
- Heavy gloves
- Screwdriver
- Wire snippers
- Electrical tape
- Utility knife
- Pry bar
- Reciprocating saw
- Backsaw
- Shop vacuum

◀ REMOVING AN INTERIOR WALL ▶

Before removing any wall, make sure it is not load bearing. If you don't know, have a structural engineer come out and examine it for you. Load bearing means that the wall is supporting part of the weight of the house, and removing a load-bearing wall without strengthening the remaining structure will cause major damage. However, if a wall is not load bearing it can easily be removed.

1 Shut off the circuit breakers that control any electrical outlets or fixtures to the area you'll be working in. Then test to make sure there is no power going to those outlets or fixtures.

2 Protect the floor with drop cloths. Cover or remove furniture in the room. Tape heavy plastic sheeting over the doorways and vents so that fine dust does not travel throughout the house.

3 Protect yourself with safety gear. Dust masks will not do the job. Invest in a respirator to protect your lungs from tiny dust particles and lead that may be in plaster walls. Wear safety goggles, heavy gloves, pants and a long-sleeved shirt, and work boots. If you're removing a plaster wall, consider wearing a body suit with an integrated hood to protect your body and hair from lead or lime dust.

4 Unscrew outlet cover plates and remove the switches or outlets. Cut the wires leading to the fixtures and wrap the ends with black electrical tape.

5 With a utility knife, score the top of the wall where it meets the ceiling (photo A). If the wall you're removing connects to a door or window, first remove the trim (photo B).

6 If you have drywall, removing it should be quick. Locate an area of the wall that's between studs and punch a hole in the wall with a pry bar or hammer. Use the clawed end or your hands (photo C) to tear out pieces of drywall from there.

7 If you have lath-and-plaster walls, the process will take a little more time and make a much bigger mess. It's best to remove the plaster first, and then the lath, rather than both at the same time. Hit the plaster with the clawed end of a pry bar to create a hole, then slide the flat end between the plaster and the lath and push up to remove it. Then remove the lath with the clawed end of the pry bar. You may be able to pull the pieces off with your hands once you make a few holes.

8 After the wall surfaces are removed, roll up any electrical wires toward the ceiling and tape them securely out of the way. If there is any plumbing in the wall, cut off the pipes at the floor and cap or reroute them.

9 Once wires and pipes are removed, you can cut out the framing with a reciprocating saw. Cut through the middle of the studs (photo D), then grab each piece and pull it back and forth until it separates from the top or bottom plate. Use a backsaw to cut out the top and bottom plates without damaging the surrounding ceiling and floor.

10 Once the large debris is out of the room, vacuum the area to remove the fine dust particles and clean off the remaining walls. Then remove the plastic sheeting and the floor and furniture coverings.

C

D

TIPS | DIY Network
Home Improvement

The Quicker Way
If you are absolutely certain there are no electrical wires or plumbing in the wall you want to remove, as Amy was with this wall that housed a pocket door, you can skip a few steps and cut through the whole thing with a reciprocating saw. If you're not sure, don't risk it.

TILE REPAIRS

You Will Need

Chisel	Putty knife
Vacuum	Grout
Thinset mortar	Sponge

PATCHING FLOOR TILE

If you remove a fixture like a toilet or vanity and find that the tile underneath is missing, you'll need to add new tile to that area. If you aren't planning to redo the floors, you'll need to find matching tiles to do the patch with (unless you already have some leftovers).

1 With a chisel, remove any loose tiles around the focused area (photo A). If there were tiles there in the past, there may also be old adhesive that needs to be scraped up. Remove any debris with a vacuum (photo B).

2 Mix a small batch of thin-set mortar. Let it sit for about 10 minutes, then apply to the area with a small putty knife (photo C).

3 Back-butter each tile individually (photo D). Place them with a bit of pressure until they are level with the existing tiles (photo E).

4 Wipe excess thinset off with a wet sponge, then gently push down on the tiles one more time.

5 Once the thinset is dry, grout the area, spreading the new grout over some of the surrounding old grout for a more seamless edge.

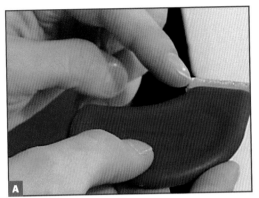

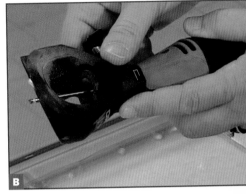

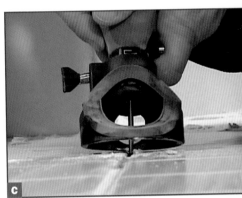

You Will Need

Rotary tool	Grout
Safety goggles	Margin float
Earplugs	Sponge

REMOVING AND REPLACING GROUT

To remove grout from small areas, a grout removal tool with a carbide blade (photo A) will do the trick. But it's slow going, so if you have four or more tiles to work around, consider renting or buying a rotary tool. Take the time to set the rotary tool to the right depth (photo B) and make sure the bit is the right size. Too big will damage the tile and too small will require more passes to remove all the grout. Slowly run the rotary tool along each grout line (photo C). If you start seeing a different color dust you're hitting a tile, so keep to the center. Also be sure to wear safety goggles and hearing protection.

1 Mix up a small batch of new grout to match the existing color (photo D). The grout should be the consistency of peanut butter.

2 Apply the grout with a margin float (photo E). It's a good idea to extend the new grout over some of the existing grout for a more seamless edge.

3 Let the grout dry for about 10 minutes. Once the tiles develop a haze, clean the excess grout off with a damp sponge.

anatomy of a wall

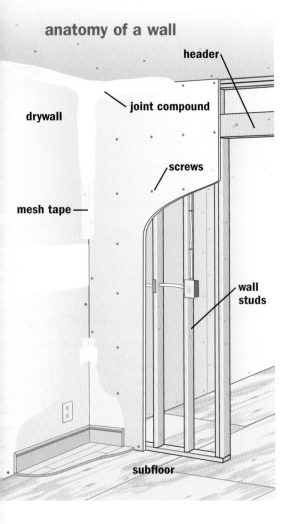

- header
- joint compound
- drywall
- screws
- mesh tape
- wall studs
- subfloor

WALLS

You Will Need

Carpenter's square	Drywall screws	Taping knife
Pencil	Self-adhesive fiberglass tape	Fine sandpaper
Drywall saw		Circular saw
1 x 3 lumber	Joint compound	Drill

PATCHING DRYWALL

Small dents and scratches in drywall can be filled with joint compound or spackle, then sanded and primed. If you have a popped nail, pry it out and nail a new one into the stud. If the existing nail won't come out or it would cause more damage to remove it, hammer in another nail right next to it so the nail head overlaps part of the existing nail. Dimple the drywall with the hammer so the nail heads sit just below the surface of the rest of the wall. Then cover with several coats of joint compound, sand and prime. Small holes can be patched with several coats of joint compound, sanded, and primed. If you have a hole between 3 and 12 inches across, use the method below.

1 Use a carpenter's square to mark straight lines around the damaged area, as it's much easier to patch a hole with straight sides. Cut out the damaged area with a drywall saw.

2 If the hole is between studs, you'll need to add a support brace to attach the new piece of drywall to (see tip). Cut a piece of 1-by-3 lumber about 8 inches longer than the hole. Put the lumber into the wall and hold it as you drive drywall screws on each side of the hole into the lumber, countersinking the screws.

3 Measure the hole and cut a new piece of drywall to fit. Attach the new piece of drywall to the support brace with countersunk drywall screws.

4 Apply self-adhesive fiberglass mesh tape to the seams.

5 Spread joint compound over the mesh tape with a taping knife. Feather the edges to reduce the amount of sanding you'll have to do. Let the joint compound dry, sand it smooth with fine sandpaper, and apply a second coat. Sand the second coat when it is dry, and then prime before painting.

TIPS | DIY Network Home Improvement

Installing a Support Brace

Drill a screw into the center of the support brace so you have something to hold on to as you screw either side in place. When the support is secure, remove the screw.

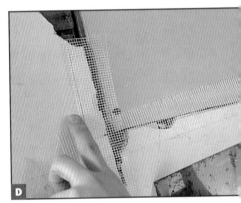

PATCHING PLASTER

Most repairs to drywall also work for plaster walls, with some exceptions. Fine cracks and nail holes can be filled with spackle. Holes up to a few inches can be filled with either drywall joint compound or patching plaster. If you cut a large hole in the wall and went through the lath, the easiest way to patch it is with a piece of drywall. Get a piece the same thickness as your current lath-and-plaster wall. If the hole is at the ceiling or floor, you can attach the drywall piece to the framing. If not, cut over to the nearest stud and attach the drywall piece to that.

1 If you're starting with a rough hole, draw lines around the perimeter (photo A) to make it a square or rectangle. Make sure the hole goes up to the nearest stud.

2 Use a circular saw to plunge-cut into the wall (photo B). This will give you relatively straight, clean edges to work with.

3 Cut a piece of drywall to fit the opening with a drywall saw or utility knife. Drill the drywall patch into the studs with 2-inch drywall screws (photo C).

4 Apply pieces of fiberglass mesh tape to span the gap between the plaster wall and the drywall patch (photo D).

5 Use a small taping knife to apply a thin layer of joint compound over the mesh tape (photo E). Feather the edges. If you don't end up with a smooth coat, let it dry, sand it lightly, and apply a second coat. Sand the second coat when it is dry, and then prime and paint.

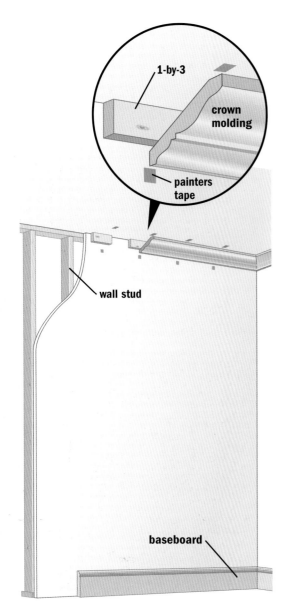

1-by-3

crown molding

painters tape

wall stud

baseboard

You Will Need

Stud finder	Drywall screws	Finish nails
Painter's tape	1 X 3 scrap lumber	Vinyl spackling
Tape measure	Coping saw	Plaster of paris
Miter saw	Nail gun or hammer and nail set	Sandpaper
Drill		Caulk

INSTALLING TRIM

Trim provides a finished look in the bathroom, and crown molding can hide bad tape or paint jobs between the wall and ceiling. Paint trim before you install it and touch up the nail holes and joints once it's in place. To do this job well, you'll need a compound miter saw. A miter box and handsaw will not give you clean, straight cuts. You can buy a compound miter saw for about $150 or rent one for a few days.

Some older homes don't have straight walls, so don't be surprised if you have to fight to get the corners of crown and baseboard trim to meet. Small gaps up to $\frac{3}{16}$ inch that occur along part of the wall between the ceiling and crown molding can be filled and caulked. It's best to use one continuous piece of molding on each wall. If you can't, cut each end at a 45-degree angle, glue the two pieces together, then sand and caulk the seam for a smooth finish. Make sure the seam falls on a stud so you have something solid to nail those pieces to. The instructions below apply to both crown and baseboard molding (except where noted). For window and door trim, simply cut the edges at a 45-degree angle and nail the trim into place on the wall.

1 Find every wall stud and mark with painter's tape just below the area that the trim will cover so you'll know where to nail once the trim is in place (see illustration).

2 For crown molding, cut 4-inch-long pieces of 1-by-3 lumber and attach them to the wall at each stud with drywall screws. This will allow you to nail the middle of the molding right into the scrap lumber as opposed to nailing into the wall and ceiling studs at the top and bottom of each piece where the carvings can get ornate. It also gives you a larger target when you're nailing the pieces in place. Baseboard can simply be installed flat against the wall.

3 Measure the walls carefully and cut the trim with a compound miter saw. It's best to cut each piece a little long at first, test in place, and keep making small cuts until it fits. Hold each section up to the wall and drill pilot holes into every other stud and within 3 inches of each end.

4 To create inside and outside corner cuts for crown molding, consult the user's guide of your compound miter saw.

5 Once you've made the cuts, dry-fit the pieces together to make sure they'll meet in the corner (photo A), then nail each piece to the wall. Use a nail gun loaded with finish nails (photo B) set so the nails will be slightly countersunk. If you use a regular hammer, stop before you hit the molding and finish the job with a nail set to countersink.

6 Fill the nail holes with vinyl spackling and sand it down to a smooth finish once it dries. Touch up each nail hole with paint. Caulk the corners. If the corner gap is too large to caulk, fill it in with plaster of paris, top with a layer of vinyl spackling, and sand until smooth. Finally, caulk the top and bottom edges for a watertight seal. Choose a caulk color that matches your trim, not the wall color around it.

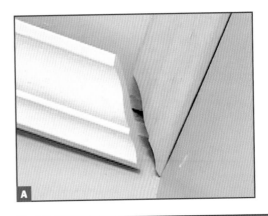
A

B

TIPS
DIY Network
Home Improvement

Painting Trim
Always paint the back and sides of your trim in addition to the front. Paint will help prevent moisture and termite damage.

cut-in

patched area

TIPS DIY Network
Home Improvement

Preparing the Roller

New rollers often have a lot of lint that can make marks on your wall. Run the roller over a few pieces of masking tape to remove the lint before you use the roller.

PAINTING

You Will Need

Drop cloths	Painters tape
TSP solution	Paint
Bucket	Small paintbrush
Sponge	Paint tray
Rags	Roller
Screwdriver	Ladder (if needed)

PAINTING A WALL

Preparing to paint takes much more time than painting, and doing it carefully is the key to a good paint job. Always buy the highest-quality paint you can. It will adhere to the wall better and possibly save you a second (or third) coat.

1 Protect your floors and furniture with drop cloths. Remove any window treatments and rods. Remove outlet covers and lighting fixtures. Tape off any areas you don't want to paint, such as baseboard or window molding. If you're replacing molding and trim, remove it before you paint the walls.

2 Wash the walls with TSP solution and look for cracks or holes. Patch any holes (see page 000) remove and replace any loose plaster (see page 000). Once you have a flat, smooth surface that's free of dust and dirt, you're ready to paint.

3 Paint one wall at a time to avoid lap marks (these appear when you let a wet edge dry and then paint the rest of the wall later). First cut in at the ceiling, sides, and floor. Cutting in means outlining the area by painting it with a brush rather than a roller.

4 To cut in, hold the brush at the base rather than at the handle for more control. Place the tips of the bristles almost to the edge of the wall. Then when you start to apply pressure, the bristles will expand out toward the edge. You want only the very tips of the outer bristles to touch the edge so you can control the amount of paint.

5 Cut in only as much area as you can finish with a roller before the paint dries. Have the roller and tray ready to go before you cut in. Dip the roller into the deep end of the tray and then roll it back and forth over the grated section to saturate the roller evenly.

6 Roll an M shape in the upper corner and then, without reloading the roller, fill in the area (see illustration, opposite page). Roll slowly and bring the roller as close to the edges as possible to mask the different texture of the area you cut in with a brush. Reload the roller when you think it is removing paint from the wall rather than adding it. Paint one 3-foot section at a time.

PAINTING A POPCORN CEILING

The trick to painting a popcorn ceiling is not to let it get too wet. Make just one pass with a roller in each section. If you miss a spot, wait until the paint is dry and then make another pass. If the popcorn does get too wet, it can start falling off in chunks. Use a segmented foam roller (shown below) for a textured ceiling. It provides more coverage on uneven areas.

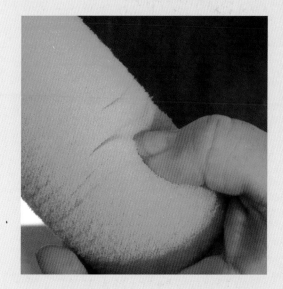

TIPS | DIY Network Home Improvement

Ladder Safety
If you need to use a ladder when painting a wall or ceiling, be sure it's set on a stable surface. Never reach when you're on a ladder. Always take the time to get down and move it over to avoid a reach.

PLUMBING

You Will Need

- 3-piece faucet set with parts
- 2 flexible water supply tubes
- Plumber's putty (if applicable)
- Adjustable wrench
- Putty knife

INSTALLING A 3-PIECE FAUCET

1 Connect a flexible water supply line to the base of each faucet (photo A). The other end will connect to the main supply line sticking out from the wall.

2 Connect another flexible supply line from each valve to the mixer (photo B).

3 To attach the faucets to the sink, remove the handles from each valve, then remove the top bezel and install from the underside of the sink. Screw the bezel back onto the valve (photo C). A rubber O-ring on the bezel eliminates the need for plumber's putty (or silicone in this case).

4 Screw the handle back on. Make sure each handle is in the off position before screwing it on.

5 To install the central spout, remove the mixer, then attach the nut and rubber washer (photo D).

6 There's no O-ring on this piece, so use plumber's putty to create a good seal. Roll the putty into a thin snake and press it against the base of the spout (photo E, next page).

7 Put the spout through the sink and attach the washer and nut (photo F, next page).

8 Reconnect the rest of the fittings and the sink is ready to install. Once it is in place, scrape off any excess putty around the fixtures with a putty knife.

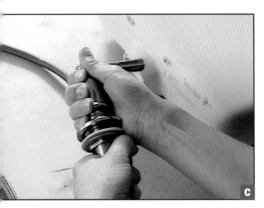

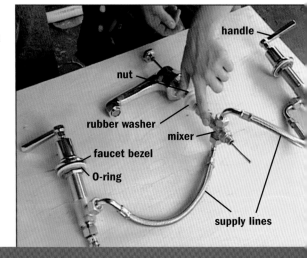

handle

nut

rubber washer

mixer

faucet bezel

O-ring

supply lines

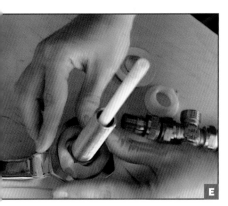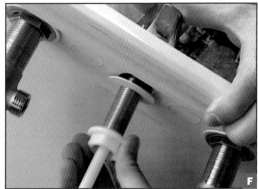

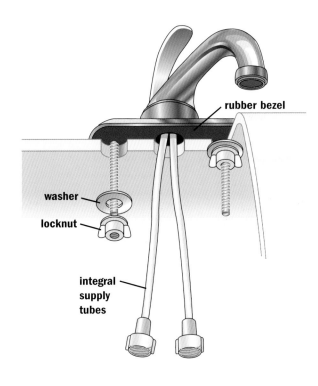

rubber bezel

washer

locknut

integral
supply
tubes

You Will Need

Plumber's putty   Adjustable wrench

Small taping knife

INSTALLING A SINGLE-LEVER FAUCET

Make sure that the faucet you buy will fit over the area you want it to cover and that the faucet's inlet shanks are spaced the same distance apart as the holes on your countertop.

1 The base of your faucet may come with a rubber bezel. If it doesn't, line the bottom with plumber's putty.

2 Place the faucet into the sink's mounting holes, make sure it's even, and press down. Use a small taping knife to remove any plumber's putty that squeezes out.

3 Use the washers and nuts that came with the faucet to lock it into place from underneath the sink. Run new flexible water supply tubes from the shutoff valves to the faucet's inlet shanks, or to the faucet's integral water supply tubes if it has them. Tighten the connections with an adjustable wrench.

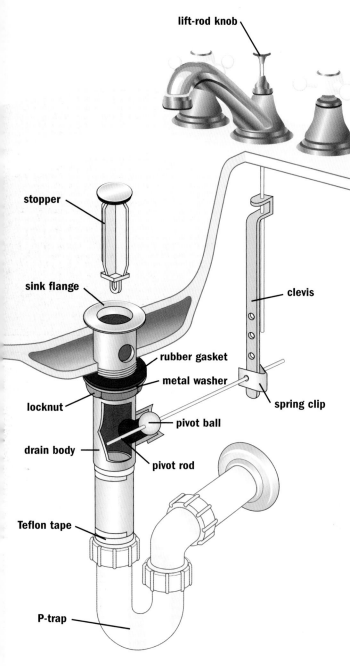

lift-rod knob

stopper

sink flange

clevis

rubber gasket

metal washer

locknut

spring clip

pivot ball

drain body

pivot rod

Teflon tape

P-trap

You Will Need

Plumber's putty

Slip-joint pliers

P-trap and couplings

INSTALLING A DRAIN AND STOPPER

1 Run a bead of plumber's putty around the edge of the sink's drain hole and press the sink flange into place.

2 Working from under the sink, take the drain body and put the locknut, followed by the metal washer, followed by the rubber gasket over one end. Screw the end with the rubber gasket onto the bottom of the flange. Use slip-joint pliers to tighten the locknut, but be careful not to overtighten it.

3 Wrap each end of the P-trap with Teflon tape and then attach one end to the drain body and the other to the waste pipe. Hand-tighten the couplings.

4 To install the pop-up stopper, first place the stopper piece into the sink flange. Now go back under the sink and hook the clevis onto the lift-rod knob, then thread the pivot rod through a hole in the clevis and into the drain body.

5 If the stopper doesn't work properly when you pull up on the lift-rod knob, move the pivot rod to another hole in the clevis and try again.

You Will Need

- Gloves
- Scraper
- Wax ring
- 4 mounting bolts
- Crescent Wrench
- 8 washers and nuts
- Plumber's putty
- Flexible water supply tube
- Mini hacksaw

◢◢◢ INSTALLING A TOILET ◣◣◣

1 Make sure the area around the drainpipe is free of any wax residue from the old ring. Install new mounting bolts in the floor flange. Then remove the rag from the drainpipe (if you had one there to prevent sewer gasses from coming in to the rom) and press a new wax ring over the flange (photo A).

2 Place the toilet on the wax ring, making sure the mounting bolts come through the holes on each side of the toilet. Press the toilet down to create a good seal with the wax ring. If you can't feel the wax ring pushing back when you lean on the toilet, or if you hear the toilet scraping against the floor, your wax ring may not be high enough. You can buy a wax ring extender at a hardware store.

3 Tighten the toilet to the floor with washers and nuts (photo B), but don't over-tighten or you might crack the porcelain. If the bolts are too long, cut them down with a mini hacksaw (photo C).

4 Put a dab of plumber's putty in the decorative caps and place them over the bolts (photo D).

5 Follow the toilet manufacturer's instructions to attach the tank to the bowl. Usually there is a rubber cushion of some type to act as a buffer between the pieces. Connect the two pieces with nuts and washers on the mounting bolts.

6 Hook up the water supply tube and open the shutoff valve. Check for leaks.

A

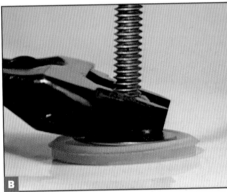

B

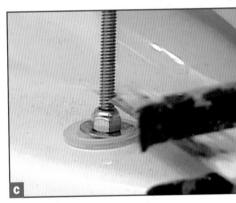

C

D

You Will Need

- 2 adjustable wrenches
- Wire brush
- Pipe-joint compound
- Flexible supply tube
- Shutoff valves
- Compression ring and slip nut (if applicable)
- Tube cutter

INSTALLING SHUTOFF VALVES

When replacing your bathroom vanity and faucet, you have a good opportunity to add shutoff valves if you don't already have them. In case of an emergency or simply to fix a leak, the water to the faucet can be stopped quickly and easily without your having to shut off water to the entire house. Shutoff valves can be angled or straight. Use straight valves for supply pipes coming out of the floor and angled for those coming out of the wall. Buy a threaded valve if you have a threaded supply pipe, or a compression valve if your supply pipe is unthreaded. You also need flexible supply tubes that will fit both your valve and fixture to tie the two together.

If you have iron or threaded pipes:

1 Shut off water to the house and drain the pipes by turning on a faucet nearest the whole-house shutoff. Disconnect the existing supply tube from the adapter and the other end from the faucet by removing the compression nut and coupling nut with an adjustable wrench.

2 Remove the old adapter from the stubout with an adjustable wrench and clean off the pipe threads with a wire brush. Slip an escutcheon over the stubout at this point if you are using one.

3 Apply pipe-joint compound to the cleaned stubout and attach the new stop valve while holding on to the stubout with a second wrench to make sure it doesn't spin.

4 Attach the new flexible supply tube to the angle-stop on the shutoff valve after you've lubricated the threads with pipe-joint compound. If you aren't using a supply tube with a threaded connector, you'll also need a compression ring and slip nut.

5 Connect the other side of the new flexible supply tube to the faucet handle with an adjustable wrench.

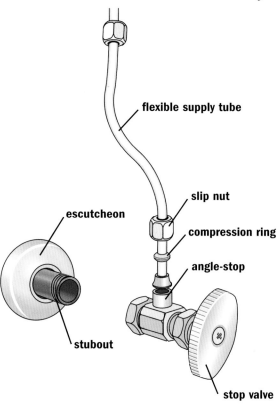

flexible supply tube

escutcheon

stubout

slip nut

compression ring

angle-stop

stop valve

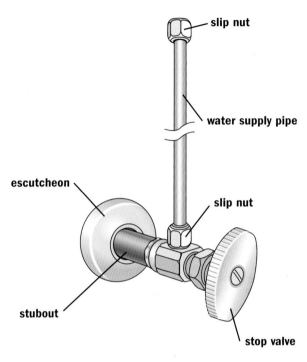

slip nut

water supply pipe

escutcheon

slip nut

stubout

stop valve

If you have copper or soldered pipes:

1 Shut off water to the house and drain the pipes by turning on a faucet nearest the whole-house shutoff. Use a tube cutter (photo A) to detach the existing water supply line from the stubout.

2 Use an adjustable wrench to disconnect the slip nut that's connecting the water supply line to the faucet.

3 Slip an escutcheon over the stubout at this point if you are using one. Apply pipe-joint compound to the threads of the new stop valve and press the valve onto the stubout. Then connect the new water supply pipe to the stop valve with a slip nut. Hold on to the stubout with a wrench as you tighten the connection.

4 Connect the other side of the new water supply line to the faucet handle using a second slip nut.

Glossary

back saw: hand saw reinforced with a metal band along its back edge

batten board: scrap piece of lumber used to establish level for setting a first course of wall tiles

beadboard: decorative panels attached vertically on a wall to protect the wall from damage and add architectural style to a room

cement: mixture of limestone and clay powder combined with water to create a solid mass; used in concrete, mortar, or grout; often referred to as portland cement

chalk line: chalk-covered string on a reel that can be pulled taught and snapped to mark straight lines on a surface

concrete: mixture of sand, water, crushed stone, and portland cement

concrete board: panels installed over subfloor or wallboard to create a strong and stable surface for floor or wall tiles

coping saw: handsaw with a thin blade used for cutting small sections out of wood

crown molding: molding installed at the top of a wall at an angle, covering the intersection of wall and ceiling

dovetail joint: a way of making a connection with two pieces of wood using interlocking mortises and tenons; technique used in well-made cabinets and furniture

dowel: a pin inserted into a hole to fasten two pieces

drywall: panels of gypsum used to finish walls and ceilings

D'VersiBit: drill bit attached to a long, flexible shaft meant to fit into tight places the drill itself cannot access

escutcheon: decorative piece that hides the gap between drywall and a pipe sticking out from the wall

feather: to blend the edges of joint compound with the surrounding wall instead of ending the edges abruptly

field tiles: tiles that fill the center area of a design, as opposed to border or accent tiles

fill stock: extra finished pieces that often come with cabinets to fill the gap between the cabinet and the wall if something prevents it from sitting flush

flux: an acid that dissolves the oxide skin off metal; used when you're about to solder two pieces of metal together

gauge rake: tool that will spread liquid material across a room to create an even depth

green board: moisture-resistant indoor tile underlayment used instead of drywall in moist areas

grout: mixture of water, cement, and sand that can be used to connect materials together (like tile) or to create a uniform surface in which to set finish materials

heat gun: specialty tool used to heat materials that have bonded to a surface, like wallpaper glue or paint, making the material easier to scrape away

impulse nailer: tool that drives nails with the pull of a trigger

jab saw: hand tool for close-quarter cutting that can be used to make plunge cuts and score materials like drywall, plywood, and plastic

joint compound: thick, spreadable substance used to fill joints in drywall

joist: steel or wood beams that support floorboards

knee wall: short wall in finished attics that supports roof rafters; also used to describe any short, non-load-bearing interior wall

lath: narrow pieces of wood used as backing for plaster or stucco walls

level: exactly horizontal

MDF: medium-density fiberboard; material made of wood fibers glued and compressed together, often used to construct veneered cabinets

miter saw: power tool that cuts narrow pieces of wood at an angle; good for cutting trim and molding

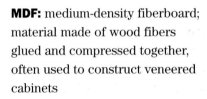

molding: wood with a carved profile, as opposed to trim, which is flat wood

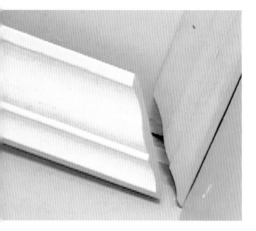

nail set: short piece of metal with a narrow blunt end that is placed on the head of a nail and then hit with a hammer; meant for counter-sinking nails

pilot hole: a predrilled hole meant to guide a nail or screw

pin nailer: pneumatic nailer that shoots tiny pins; good for small-scale craft and wood projects

plumb: exactly vertical

plunge cut: to cut directly into the center of an area

PVC: a polymer of vinyl chloride that can be molded into forms such as pipes

skim coat: a thin layer of joint compound or gypsum and spackle applied to a wall to smooth out any rough spots

slake: the process that occurs when mortar is allowed to rest after mixing with water

solder: to join two metal surfaces together

stubout: the section of pipe that sticks out through the finished wall

studs: usually 2 x 4 or 2 x 6 wood beams that make up the interior frame of a wall

subfloor: boards laid over joists to support the finish floor

thinset mortar: a strong mortar designed to adhere well in a thin layer; used for adhering tile to walls and subfloors

wet saw: electric saw whose blade is constantly sprayed with water during cutting to keep it cool; uses a diamond blade to cut through ceramic as well as stone

wet wall: a wall that contains plumbing

Photography Credits

All photographs are courtesy of DIY Network unless otherwise credited.

COURTESY OF AMERICAN STANDARD
(www.americanstandard.com):
16 bottom (photo by Earl Kendall, Earl
Kendall Photographs), 26, 28 left, 28 right,
29 top right, 29 top left, 29 bottom right,
30 top, 31 bottom, 31 top, 32 top, 35 top,
37 bottom right, 38 top right (photo by
Keller & Keller), 38 left, 44 top, 44 middle,
44 left, 45 bottom, 46 right, 46 top right,
47 top, 51 top, 51 bottom, 52 bottom,
52 top, 54 bottom left, 54 bottom right,
54 top, 55 bottom, 56 left, 57 bottom right

COURTESY OF ARISTOKRAFT CABINETRY
(www.aristokraft.com): 33 left, 40,
41 bottom

COURTESY OF ARMSTRONG RESILIENT FLOORING
(Highland Park Collection, Eldoret Green
Mist 97002, www.armstrong.com): 36

BOB DURLAND: 8

COURTESY OF FIRED EARTH
(www.firedearth.com): 25 right, 34 top, 39
top, 43 bottom, 48 left, 48 right, 57 top left

COURTESY OF KOHLER COMPANY
(www.kohler.com): 27, 30 bottom,
32 bottom left, 34 bottom, 36 top left,
49 bottom, 50 right, 53, 57 bottom left

COURTESY OF LASCO BATHWARE
(www.lascobathware.com):
6, 24, 35 bottom, 50 left, 56 right

COURTESY OF MOEN
(www.moen.com): 22 left, 25 top left,
33 right, 36 bottom left, 42 right, 45 top,
46 left, 49 top

COURTESY OF PORCHER
(www.porcher.com): 47 bottom (photo by
Earl Kendall, Earl Kendall Photographs)

COURTESY OF WILSONART SOLID SURFACE
(www.wilsonartsolidsurface.com): 42 left

Acknowledgements

Amy would like to thank Freddy James and
everyone at DIY Network for their support from
the very beginning; Steve Edelman for his vision
and guidance; John Kitchener, Emily Burton,
Mary Kay Reistad, and the entire "Bathroom
Team" at Edelman Productions (you rock);
Mark Torgeson and Shane Kretzsinger, my
friends and contractors, for their expertise,
long hours, and all the laughter; Bob Durland
and Eric Klang for always getting the shot; the
team at Arron Stokes; my family for their love
and humor; and Michael Egan, my husband
and best friend, for encouraging me toward
this adventure in the first place.

Index

Metric Conversion Table

Inches	Decimal Inches	Rounded Metric	Inches	Decimal Inches	Rounded Metric	Inches	Decimal Inches	Rounded Metric
1/16	.0625	1.6 mm/.16 cm	7½	7.5	19 cm	18		45.7 cm
1/8	.0125	3 mm/.3 cm	7¾	7.75	19.7 cm	18¼	18.25	46.4 cm
3/16	.1875	5 mm/.5 cm	8		20.3 cm	18½	18.5	47 cm
¼	.25	6 mm/.6 cm	8¼	8.25	21 cm	18¾	18.75	47.6 cm
5/16	.3125	8 mm/.8 cm	8½	8.5	21.6 cm	19		48.3 cm
3/8	.375	9.5 mm/.95 cm	8¾	8.75	22.2 cm	19¼	19.25	48.9 cm
7/16	.4375	1.1 cm	9		22.9 cm	19½	19.5	49.5 cm
½	.5	1.3 cm	9¼	9.25	23.5 cm	19¾	19.75	50.2 cm
9/16	.5625	1.4 cm	9½	9.5	24.1 cm	20		50.8 cm
5/8	.625	1.6 cm	9¾	9.75	24.8 cm	20¼	20.25	51.4 cm
11/16	.6875	1.7 cm	10		25.4 cm	20½	20.5	52.1 cm
¾	.75	1.9 cm	10¼	10.25	26 cm	20¾	20.75	52.7 cm
13/16	.8125	2.1 cm	10½	10.5	26.7 cm	21		53.3 cm
7/8	.875	2.2 cm	10¾	10.75	27.3 cm	21¼	21.25	54 cm
15/16	.9375	2.4 cm	11		27.9 cm	21½	21.5	54.6 cm
			11¼	11.25	28.6 cm	21¾	21.75	55.2 cm
1		2.5 cm	11½	11.5	29.2 cm	22		55.9 cm
1¼	1.25	3.2 cm	11¾	11.75	30 cm	22¼	22.25	56.5 cm
1½	1.5	3.8 cm	12		30.5 cm	22½	22.5	57.2 cm
1¾	1.75	4.4 cm	12¼	12.25	31.1 cm	22¾	22.75	57.8 cm
2		5 cm	12½	12.5	31.8 cm	23		58.4 cm
2¼	2.25	5.7 cm	12¾	12.75	32.4 cm	23¼	23.25	59 cm
2½	2.5	6.4 cm	13		33 cm	23½	23.5	59.7 cm
2¾	2.75	7 cm	13¼	13.25	33.7 cm	23¾	23.75	60.3 cm
3		7.6 cm	13½	13.5	34.3 cm	24		61 cm
3¼	3.25	8.3 cm	13¾	13.75	35 cm	24¼	24.25	61.6 cm
3½	3.5	8.9 cm	14		35.6 cm	24½	24.5	62.2 cm
3¾	3.75	9.5 cm	14¼	14.25	36.2 cm	24¾	24.75	62.9 cm
4		10.2 cm	14½	14.5	36.8 cm	25		63.5 cm
4¼	4.25	10.8 cm	14¾	14.75	37.5 cm	25¼	25.25	64.1 cm
4½	4.5	11.4 cm	15		38.1 cm	25½	25.5	64.8 cm
4¾	4.75	12 cm	15¼	15.25	38.7 cm	25¾	25.75	65.4 cm
5		12.7 cm	15½	15.5	39.4 cm	26		66 cm
5¼	5.25	13.3 cm	15¾	15.75	40 cm	26¼	26.25	66.7 cm
5½	5.5	14 cm	16		40.6 cm	26½	26.5	67.3 cm
5¾	5.75	14.6 cm	16¼	16.25	41.3 cm	26¾	26.75	68 cm
6		15.2 cm	16½	16.5	41.9 cm	27		68.6 cm
6¼	6.25	15.9 cm	16¾	16.75	42.5 cm	27¼	27.25	69.2 cm
6½	6.5	16.5 cm	17		43.2 cm	27½	27.5	69.9 cm
6¾	6.75	17.1 cm	17¼	17.25	43.8 cm	27¾	27.75	70.5 cm
7		17.8 cm	17½	17.5	44.5 cm	28		71.1 cm
7¼	7.25	18.4 cm	17¾	17.75	45.1 cm			